T0277921

SIERRA
GRAND TRAVERSE

SIERRA
GRAND TRAVERSE

An Epic Route Across the Range of Light

JOHN CHAPMAN AND MONICA CHAPMAN

MOUNTAINEERS
BOOKS

MOUNTAINEERS BOOKS is dedicated to the exploration, preservation, and enjoyment of outdoor and wilderness areas.

1001 SW Klickitat Way, Suite 201, Seattle, WA 98134
800-553-4453, www.mountaineersbooks.org

Printed in China
Distributed in the United Kingdom by Cordee, www.cordee.co.uk

First edition, 2023

Copyeditor: Ginger Oppenheimer
Design and layout: Jen Grable
All maps, photographs, and elevation profiles by the authors, unless credited otherwise
Cover photographs, front: *Sunset in Sixty Lake Basin* (Section 4); back, *Red and White Mountain from Laurel Creek* (Section 2)
Frontispiece: *Evening at Banner Peak, Thousand Island Lake* (Section 1)

The background shading for these maps was produced using map viewer CalTopo. For more information, visit caltopo.com.

Library of Congress Cataloging-in-Publication Data is on file for this title at https://lccn.loc.gov/2022039330. The LC ebook record is available at https://lccn.loc.gov/2022039331.

Mountaineers Books titles may be purchased for corporate, educational, or other promotional sales, and our authors are available for a wide range of events. For information on special discounts or booking an author, contact our customer service at 800-553-4453 or mbooks@ mountaineersbooks.org.

Printed on FSC-certified materials

ISBN (paperback): 978-1-68051-618-0
ISBN (ebook): 978-1-68051-619-7

An independent nonprofit publisher since 1960

CONTENTS

SECTION 1: TUOLUMNE MEADOWS TO HORSESHOE LAKE

SECTION 2: HORSESHOE LAKE TO PIUTE PASS

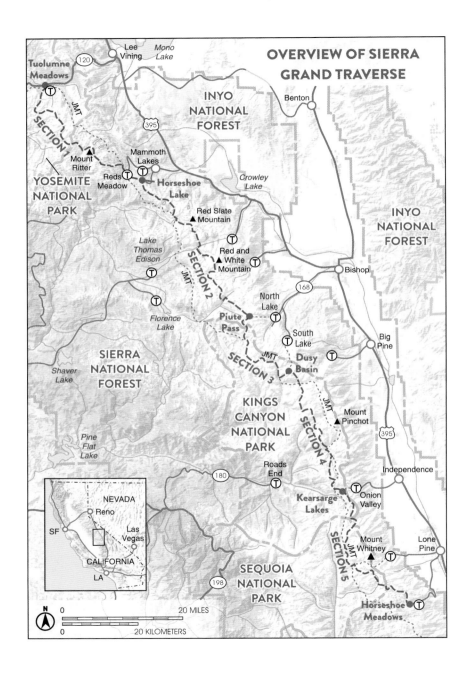

SECTION 3: PIUTE PASS TO DUSY BASIN

SECTION 4: DUSY BASIN TO KEARSARGE LAKES

SECTION 5: KEARSARGE LAKES TO HORSESHOE MEADOWS

TRAVERSE AT A GLANCE

TRAIL LEG	DISTANCE (miles)	ELEVATION GAIN/LOSS (feet)	HIKING TIME (hours)
SECTION 1. TUOLUMNE MEADOWS TO HORSESHOE LAKE			
1. Tuolumne Meadows to Nelson Lake	7.3	1850 / 820	3½–4½
2. Nelson Lake to Ireland Lake	5.6	2190 / 1060	5–6
3. Ireland Lake to Hutchings Basin	6.5	1880 / 2110	8–11
4. Hutchings Basin to North Fork San Joaquin River	4.8	2440 / 2840	7½–9
5. North Fork San Joaquin River to Thousand Island Lake	4.8	2070 / 2340	6½–8
6. Thousand Island Lake to Minaret Lake	6	1620 / 1660	6–7½
7. Minaret Lake to Reds Meadow	7.7	120 / 2270	3–4
8. Reds Meadow to Horseshoe Lake	4.2	1670 / 420	2–2½
SECTION 2. HORSESHOE LAKE TO PIUTE PASS			
1. Horseshoe Lake to Deer Lakes	6.8	2500 / 710	3½–4½
2. Deer Lakes to Pika Lake	2.6	610 / 770	2–2½
3. Pika Lake to Lake Virginia	4.8	1540 / 1730	5½–8
4. Lake Virginia to Tully Lake	4.9	1180 / 930	3–4
5. Tully Lake to Mono Creek	5.5	1280 / 3030	5½–6½
6. Mono Creek to Upper Mills Lake	4.8	2590 / 220	4–5
7. Upper Mills Lake to Black Bear Lake	6.4	2240 / 2150	7–9
8. Black Bear Lake to Elba Lake	7.5	2290 / 2590	7–8½
9. Elba Lake to Piute Pass	5.5	1320 / 840	4–5

TRAIL LEG	DISTANCE (miles)	ELEVATION GAIN/LOSS (feet)	HIKING TIME (hours)
SECTION 3. PIUTE PASS TO DUSY BASIN			
1. Piute Pass to Darwin Bench	6.3	1030 / 1210	6–9
2. Darwin Bench to Wanda Lake	5.4	780 / 600	3–4½
3. Wanda Lake to Unnamed Lake	4.7	530 / 1110	3½–4½
4. Unnamed Lake to Le Conte Ranger Station	4.3	50 / 2150	2½–3
5. Le Conte Ranger Station to Dusy Basin	3.8	2680 / 50	4–5
SECTION 4. DUSY BASIN TO KEARSARGE LAKES			
1. Dusy Basin to Glacier Creek	4.7	600 / 3080	6–7½
2. Glacier Creek to Dumbbell Lakes	3.9	2620 / 620	6–8
3. Dumbbell Lakes to Bench Lake	7.7	2820 / 3260	9–10
4. Bench Lake to Window Lake	5.6	1940 / 1800	6½–7½
5. Window Lake to Sixty Lake Basin	5.7	2210 / 2260	5½–6½
6. Sixty Lake Basin to Kearsarge Lakes	9.6	2170 / 1820	8–9
SECTION 5. KEARSARGE LAKES TO HORSESHOE MEADOWS			
1. Kearsarge Lakes to Golden Bear Lake	4.1	1440 / 1260	5–6
2. Golden Bear Lake to Shepherd Pass	6.5	2700 / 1860	7½–9
3. Shepherd Pass to Wright Lakes	4.3	560 / 1430	3½–4
4. Wright Lakes to Crabtree Ranger Station	7.4	780 / 1280	4–4½
5. Crabtree Ranger Station to Sky Blue Lake	7.2	2450 / 1560	7–9
6. Sky Blue Lake to Cottonwood Lake 3	6.6	1450 / 1900	5½–6½
7. Cottonwood Lake 3 to Horseshoe Meadows	6.5	50 / 1110	2½–3

INTRODUCTION

One of the world's most scenic mountain ranges, the Sierra Nevada features a sea of craggy peaks and a multitude of pristine alpine lakes. Running north–south for four hundred miles in California east of the Central Valley, it has abundant wildflowers, meadow-filled valleys, and many well-maintained trails. The highest parts of the range are undeveloped and have become a mecca for experienced backpackers seeking a wilderness experience.

John Muir aptly described the Sierra Nevada as the "Range of Light." Unlike in many other mountain ranges, from midsummer through early fall, the weather in the Sierra is generally mild, with the occasional midday thunderstorm, and the range's north-south orientation results in many opportunities to view glorious sunrises and sunsets that feature glowing rock faces reflected in calm lakes. This common phenomenon, called alpenglow, is one of the top reasons so many hikers love the High Sierra.

The Sierra Grand Traverse passes through five wilderness areas spread across three national parks and two national forests. This rigorous traverse of the range runs from Tuolumne Meadows south past Mount Whitney to Horseshoe Meadows. Not an easy backpack along well-defined trails, it is best suited for experienced hikers with solid navigation skills. It crosses many miles of scree (loose rocks) and boulder fields and descends and climbs steeply over high passes that lack trails, but the rewards are great—it visits some of the best wilderness in the Sierra Nevada. Walking its entire length, about two hundred miles, takes between twenty-five and forty-five days, depending on the type of experience you seek, the amount of time you can devote to it, and how far you are prepared to walk each day.

This demanding hike crosses forty-one passes, thirty-one of which require well-honed navigation skills. About 80 percent is on or above tree line and 60 percent is cross-country. Even though the entire traverse involves 56,000 feet of

Tarn near Cotton Lake (Section 2)

elevation gain and loss, not all of it is overly steep as it visits thirty scenic lake basins. Starting at 8580 feet in Tuolumne Meadows, the route drops below that elevation only twice. Most of the time it stays between 9000 feet and 12,000 feet.

The trail description has been divided into five sections, each starting and ending at resupply points. Those sections are then subdivided into thirty-six legs, bookended by clearly defined destinations such as lakes, passes, meadows, and more. Apart from Mammoth Lakes, all the other access points require at least half a day's walk to the nearest road. This guide provides detailed topographic maps and elevation charts of the entire route.

Compared to other recognized trails and routes in the Sierra Nevada, this traverse spends less time on trails, has more miles above tree line, crosses more passes, and visits more lakes. It features spectacular scenery and many beautiful lake basins, highlighting the range's grand scenery, hence the name: Sierra Grand Traverse.

While the Sierra Grand Traverse can be undertaken in either direction, there are some advantages of walking north to south as we describe in this guide. (The Sierra actually run north-northwest to south-southeast, rather than true north to south.) The range is a little lower in elevation in the north, which assists with acclimatization on the entire traverse since the passes on the southern end have higher elevations. Another advantage of traveling north to south is that the passes without trails are easier to traverse (see Tips for Cross-country Travel in Preparation & Planning for details). We walked some sections in both directions and found the north to south option better. Traveling in this direction also leaves the ascent of Mount Whitney as a highlight near the end of the trip.

In such a large range, variations to the Sierra Grand Traverse are possible. On some sections you really have no choice, such as when following the John Muir Trail across Muir Pass—any other alternative across Goddard Divide is not logical as it would be a winding route with large ascents and descents crossing difficult passes. Where backpackers have several options, we describe the most scenic route, which often heads through a lovely lake basin.

The Sierra Grand Traverse is not the highest possible traverse in the range, which includes multiple class 3 and 4 passes. Such passes require some climbing experience and are beyond the skill of many hikers. The Sierra Grand Traverse minimizes class 3 sections and instead passes through many beautiful lake basins, highlighting the extraordinary scenery of the Sierra Nevada.

On our first trip to the Sierra Nevada, we walked the Sierra High Route designed by Steve Roper. An excellent route, it strays away from some of the

Sunset on Cirque Crest, Lake Basin (Section 4)

higher lake basins to follow easier trails. Plus, it does not pass near Mount Whitney, the highest peak in the range.

Inspired by the Sierra High Route but lured by scenic features, we designed the Sierra Grand Traverse to include more high lake basins and a side trip to Mount Whitney. It crosses multiple Grade 2 passes and is suitable for experienced hikers without climbing experience. None of it is new: Others have explored all of the passes and lake basins, and we benefited from their knowledge in piecing together this route. Some parts of the traverse follow existing trails and routes. Notably about one-third (66 miles) follows the Sierra High Route and 29 miles follow the John Muir Trail, but the majority of the Sierra Grand Traverse is cross-country. Our aim was to traverse the range from Tuolumne Meadows, south past Mount Whitney to Horseshoe Meadows while staying mainly on or above tree line and visiting some of the most scenic areas of the High Sierra.

The traverse passes through spectacular scenery in three national parks and two national forests. Almost the entire route stays within five wilderness areas

Leaving Hutchings Basin (Section 1)

without vehicle access or development. While about the same length as the Sierra High Route, the Sierra Grand Traverse stays at higher elevations on average, crosses more passes, visits more lake basins, and has less trail walking, making it an epic route across the Range of Light.

OVERVIEW OF THE REGION

Long explored, exploited, and revered, the Sierra Nevada has both suffered and benefited from human presence. American Indians lived in and explored the Sierra Nevada, as far back as ten thousand years. Tribes exchanged items that were common in one region for items plentiful in another. The various tribes regularly crossed the Sierra crest for trade purposes using multiple passes, even building summer shelters in some passes. Tools and evidence of tool making have been found on the summits of some Sierra peaks, so they did indeed explore all of the range. Over thousands of years, tribal boundaries and tribes probably changed, but when Europeans arrived in the 1800s, the eastern side of the range was occupied by the Paiutes and Mono Indians, while the Western Mono, Miwok, and Yurok tribes occupied the west side.

Spanish explorers and missionaries arrived in the 1700s and began working to convert the Indigenous populations to Christianity. They also brought diseases, but because they did not venture far inland, those illnesses had little effect on the local Sierra tribes. That all changed in the early 1860s when European settlers occupied parts of the Owens Valley, west of the Sierra crest, and treated the local inhabitants as though they did not exist. The Paiute tribe's main food source was grain grown on small plots of irrigated land. The settlers' cattle devoured these plots along with many other plants in the valley. In desperation, a starving Paiute killed a cow, and in retaliation, settlers killed a Paiute. The killing escalated and the Europeans set about exterminating the American Indians who remained. Many were marched off to a reservation; the rest were hunted and often killed. While people think of the High Sierra as wilderness, in reality it was part of the homeland of many humans for thousands of years.

As European settlement advanced, the easy-to-reach, fertile valleys were soon filled with ranches. With easy access to the High Sierra, some ranchers began using the high meadows to graze their sheep in summer. Sheep eat everything, resulting in overgrazing of these meadows. The sheepherders' solution was to simply move the sheep to the next meadow and repeat the cycle. Alpine vegetation grows and recovers slowly, and some damage from the sheepherding era is still evident today. The practice was taken up by a man who would go on to influence the entire region: John Muir. In 1849, as a youngster, he immigrated from Scotland to Wisconsin. He was gifted and observant; his studies focused on botany and geology. After an accident in which he almost lost his eyesight, he decided to travel more. Among other adventures, he trekked a thousand miles from Kentucky

Heading toward Amelia Earhart Pass (Section 1)

to Florida before turning his attention west: to California. Muir visited Yosemite Valley in the late 1860s, and like many people since, was awestruck.

When Muir began herding sheep at Tuolumne Meadows, he was shocked by the damage he saw from grazing. He resided in Yosemite Valley for a few years and proposed that the valley was formed by glaciation, publishing his work and cementing his reputation in the scientific community. He explored the range and made the first recorded ascent of Mount Ritter. Muir traveled to other areas and began writing extensively, establishing himself as an early conservationist in the United States. Well-known people visited his simple home, and in 1890 he was able to persuade the most powerful people in the country to create Yosemite National Park, although the park did not include Yosemite Valley until 1903. In 1892, he founded the Sierra Club, which became instrumental in the creation of new parks and national forests, and he also helped increase protection of existing national parks. John Muir was the catalyst for the creation of the many national parks and wilderness areas in the US.

However, John Muir was not the only one exploring the Sierra Nevada. Starting with surveyors, then explorers, who roamed the range, people have been traversing these mountains for decades. Some of the features in the Central Sierra are named after these early visitors. Josiah Whitney was the leader of the California Geological Survey; the highest peak in the range—Mount Whitney—is named for him. The King River is named after a young surveyor, Clarence King, who became entranced with the range and explored it widely. Sheepherders visited most of the range but left few records of their passing; an exception was Frank Dusy who is remembered by Dusy Basin. In the 1870s others began exploring for the sake of it, including Frederick Henry Wales, W. B. Wallace, and J. W. A. Wright, who visited the Kern River plateau east of Mount Whitney; lakes and streams there are named after them.

In the 1880s Theodore Solomons came up with an idea for a trail along the range and began exploring ways to connect areas. The route from the Mount Ritter area to Kings Canyon he described as a "journey fit for gods," an apt description. He called the scenery in the Bears Lakes basin "striking." He named Evolution Lake, describing it as the "finest paradise" he had ever seen, and then named all the peaks around it—Darwin, Spencer, Huxley, and Fiske—after prominent philosophers and scientists of the time. A year later, in 1895 he explored Mono Creek and described the four U-shaped side valleys as "magnificent alpine recesses."

Mount Spencer and tarn near Evolution Lake (Section 3)

Perhaps the most prolific explorer of the High Sierra was Joseph Le Conte who, between 1892 and 1930, made forty-four extended trips. He drew maps and named Marion Lake after his wife. Muir Pass is named after John Muir, of course, and the lakes on either side of it are named after his daughters Wanda and Helen. Some explorers preferred to name features after their appearance or characteristics. Bolton Brown named Arrow Peak and Split Mountain. Other examples of appearances leading to their current names are Sixty Lake Basin, Thousand Island Lake, Red and White Mountain, Slate Mountain, White Rock Pass, Dumbbell Lakes, and Cataract Creek. Others have been named after fauna such as Deer Lakes, Duck Lake, Pika Lake, Bear Lakes, and Deer Meadow.

For most features you'll encounter, we've used the place names that appear on the US Geological Survey (USGS) maps. The maps in this guide also use a variety of unofficial place names commonly used in other books and on websites. For a few places that did not seem to have widely accepted official or unofficial names, we named a few to make the trail descriptions easier to use, including Reymann Pass, Amelia Earhart Pass, Mine Site, Lower Dusy Basin, and Upper Window Lake.

Climate
The Sierra Nevada has four distinct seasons. Summer is mostly dry with mild temperatures, and from July to mid-September most days are sunny. The most common wet weather events in summer are afternoon thunderstorms. If thunderstorm clouds are building, set up camp early to avoid being out in the open and reduce your risk of a lightning strike. One or two large storms, lasting up to four days, sweep through each summer. Ensure you're equipped with full wet weather clothing and a suitable tent because summer storms, while rare, can occur anytime.

Summer ends abruptly in early to mid-September when the temperature drops noticeably, often heralded by the first winter-like storm. The cold, fine days can provide excellent walking conditions, although frosty mornings can make some passes challenging. In winter, the Sierra Nevada can receive heavy snowfalls with drifts 50 feet high. In spring, the heavy snow cover starts to melt, raising water levels in most streams, which makes off-trail travel difficult. Some streams stay at peak levels well into late July in a heavy snow year.

Geology
The four hundred miles of the Sierra run parallel to the California coast. While the western edge of the range slopes gently, the eastern side is a steep scarp that

Scree-covered White Fork Pass (Section 4)

falls 10,000 feet to the Owens Valley. The plateau is not flat: Glaciers and erosion have dissected the range into a series of valleys. The lower slopes of the range have been modified extensively by human development. However, the jewel is the high country, which has been managed as wilderness and is protected in a series of national parks and national forests. The crest of the range rises slowly from north to south to culminate at Mount Whitney, the highest point in the contiguous United States at 14,505 feet.

Polished granite slabs, colorful cliffs, and peaks that sport extensive bands of scree dominate most views. The major bedrock is granite, a common name for a range of plutonic rocks. Granite rocks are composed of crystals that form when molten minerals cool slowly. Between one hundred million and sixty million years ago, a huge reservoir of magma formed below modern-day California. A massive amount of heat from this magma changed the overlying older rocks, often making them harder, well below the surface. Over millions of years the granite rose slowly and most of the overlying rock eroded; for a long time the range was a series of low hills. About five million years ago, the rising accelerated, creating a high mountain range. On this higher range, glaciers became a powerful erosive force that left behind the U-shaped high valleys now dotted with meadows and lakes. The main era of glaciation ended around ten thousand years ago when the climate warmed. Around one thousand years ago, a mini ice age began, allowing some small glaciers to develop. These glaciers, formed in the highest valleys, carved regions that are now rock-bound lakes backed by steep cirques. Some of these small glaciers and semi-permanent snowfields remain, although they are all receding due to more recent changes in the climate.

While granite is the dominant rock type, outcrops of many other rock types exist in the range. Between fifteen million and five million years ago, as the granite bedrock rose, it fractured along a series of fault lines. The most obvious is on the eastern side of the range where the escarpment drops steeply to the Owens Valley. Various volcanoes then formed and erupted, depositing volcanic material over the range and filling some valleys. Volcanic activity continued to occur spasmodically, and around 760,000 years ago a huge volcanic eruption created the Long Valley Caldera. This event, more than three thousand times more powerful than the eruption of Mount St. Helens in Washington State in 1980, left behind a huge basin east of the town of Mammoth Lakes. Volcanic activity continued in that region, and Mammoth Mountain is the remains of a volcano that was active from around 110,000 to 60,000 years ago. More recently, from Mammoth Mountain north to Mono Lake, a line of small craters has risen as a result of volcanic activity that took place until as recently as six hundred years ago.

In general volcanic rocks erode more easily than granite and can soon vanish. Remnants from volcanic activity exist in various places. The hexagonal basalt columns of Devils Postpile are the best example along the Sierra Grand Traverse.

Metamorphic rocks are sedimentary rocks that have been altered by heat from the underlying granite mass, which often makes them harder. Such outcrops commonly occur on some of the higher peaks as colorful red, brown, and green bands in exposed cliffs. On the Sierra Grand Traverse, you'll see clear examples of metamorphic rocks in places such as the Ritter Range, Red and White Mountain, and the high basin east of Vernon Pass.

While most of the glaciers have melted, their effect on landforms is obvious. U-shaped valleys, hanging side valleys, and curved cirques on the sides of higher peaks are common. Lake basins are one of the most obvious landforms created by glaciation. Granite is a dense rock that holds water well. Combine granite landforms with the carving action of glaciers, and you'll discover how so many lakes formed in the High Sierra. These scenic lakes provide not just beautiful scenery but a permanent water supply for backpackers and hikers.

Flora

The Sierra Grand Traverse rarely drops below 9000 feet, and so the vegetation zones it passes through are primarily subalpine or alpine. Both zones have short summers and long severe winters featuring strong winds. While there is plenty of snow in winter, the normally dry summers have led to plants that grow and flower quickly while keeping water loss to a minimum. Narrow pine needles minimize surface area, while plants with broad leaves often have fine white hairs that reflect sunlight and slow air movement. Some plants hug the ground to limit their exposure to wind and conserve water.

The subalpine zone, which ranges from around 8000 to 11,000 feet and is below tree line, features mainly open woodland composed mostly of pines. To reduce water loss by evaporation, pines have fine needle-like leaves and small pinecones. Under the trees the forest floor is fairly open and generally easy to walk through. As a result of the severe climate, trees grow slowly. Large trees can be more than five hundred years old, and stands of single species are rare. Lodgepole pines grow in the lower part of this zone. Their needles, which grow in pairs, are twisted. Western white pines have long needles in bunches of five, and foxtail pines have shorter needles, also in bunches of five, that grow more densely and look like a foxtail. Mountain hemlock, the most common tree in this zone, has tightly bunched, upward-curving needles near the twig ends. Whitebark pine, the most widespread species, has short needles in bunches of five like the western white and foxtail. On the tree line, whitebark is often the dominant species, and it sometimes occurs in isolated stands well above the main tree line.

Below tree line, the subalpine zone includes some open meadows, areas that are usually wet during the spring melt, inhibiting tree growth. The flat bases of glacier-carved valleys typically contain meadows with bands of trees growing on the steep valley sides. Some examples of subalpine meadows include Rafferty Creek, Horse Heaven near Tully Hole, Deer Meadow, and Cottonwood Lakes. Grasses and sedges are the most common plants in meadows, and they usually have small flowers. Unlike the strappy leaves of sedges, grasses never have three-sided leaves, but to identify the species of either plant you need to examine its seeds. You will find many other plants with showy flowers often in sheltered locations. The paintbrush family of flowers ranges from pink to bright red, and with

Wildflowers, clockwise from top left: gentian; sunflower; monkeyflower; cutleaf daisies; lupine, alpine columbine; red columbine; paintbrush

stems up to three feet high, they are fairly common. Red columbine, also common, has distinctive, long, narrow nectar tubes on the back of the flower. Gentian are a pitcher flower that trap insects. These bright blue flowers stand upright, have a wide tube below the flower, and often have stripes and spots to lure insects inside. Yellow flowers abound as well. Many are members of the Asteraceae family, which includes sunflowers and daisies. The obvious outer petals are classified as ray petals, while the real flowers are the tiny clusters in the center. You'll also see monkeyflowers, especially alongside streambeds; yellow is the most common. Part of the monkeyflower blossom closes when it has been touched, which helps to trap pollen from visiting insects.

The alpine zone is above tree line. In the north, tree line is around 10,000 feet and above, while farther south around Mount Whitney, the tree line rises to around 11,000 feet. The alpine zone contains more than six hundred species of flowering plants, and while some species are locally dominant, there aren't any species common across the entire range.

The subalpine flowers that grow in the alpine zone are typically from the same family but have evolved to cope with the changed conditions. Generally these varieties have shorter stems and are sometimes less colorful than those in the subalpine zone. The alpine columbine, for example, looks similar to the red columbine but has a shorter stem, is pink to white, and is pollinated by moths instead of hummingbirds.

Higher up, scree and exposed bedrock dominate since they have not yet eroded to soil. Even there, tough plants exist with some, such as lupines, exhibiting showy flowers. On the highest passes and peaks, the striking blue sky pilot grows in talus and almost bare rock.

Willow grows in both zones, mainly around creeks and in drainage lines, forming dense thickets up to ten feet high, which can be challenging to walk through. When you encounter a willow thicket, it is usually easier to take the long way around.

Wildlife

The subalpine and alpine zones support a multitude of life. The most common life form in the Sierra Nevada, insects often go unnoticed until they annoy humans. Important for the environment since most flowers are pollinated by insects, this life form is at the bottom of the food chain and includes dragonflies, damselflies, grasshoppers, crickets, beetles, bees, ants, wasps, and flies. Perhaps the least loved insects are mosquitoes; the females bite mammals, including humans, to obtain

California tortoiseshell butterfly

proteins from blood for breeding. Mosquito numbers peak in early to midsummer and their populations vary annually by time and location. One meadow may harbor swarms of biting insects while the next has hardly any. Other biting insects you may encounter are gnats, black files, and ticks. Insect repellent, long sleeves, light long-legged pants, and an insect net for your head reduce your chances of being bitten.

More than one hundred species of butterflies and moths flutter around the flowers and grasses in the meadows. Many of these fliers are dull in appearance, often in shades of orange, yellow, or white with black bars or dots, which forms an effective camouflage. Distinguishing between moths and butterflies can be challenging. While both can rest with outstretched wings, moths sometimes rest with their wings at an angle, while butterflies sometimes rest with their wings held together in a vertical position. Another difference: Moths can fly at night while butterflies fly in daylight only.

In the insect world, spiders are a feared predator. A variety of spiders hunt and capture prey by stalking or ambushing, and an astonishing number of this type inhabit Sierra meadows. Other spiders snare prey by catching them in their sticky webs. You do not need to worry about spiders; most are harmless to humans and hide when you enter their territory.

The Sierra Nevada has many high lakes and, historically, most of them did not contain fish. The numerous high waterfalls and rugged canyons presented natural barriers that prevented fish migration upstream to high elevation. Starting in the mid-1800s, however, trout were introduced to the high lakes and many lakes were then regularly stocked with fingerlings. In 1991 the practice of stocking lakes in national parks ceased, although it continues in national forests. Trout are an efficient aquatic predator and have significantly reduced some native aquatic species. Once lakes have been stocked, ending the practice reduces but does not eliminate the fish population. A program is underway to remove trout from around

19 percent of all the high lakes, executed with a combination of techniques that includes gill nets and electrofishing. We passed two lakes where this process was taking place; signage explained the visible net line. In other lakes the process had been completed, and success is marked by the return of two species of endangered mountain yellow-legged frogs. A majority of the high lakes still contain trout, so there are ample opportunities for people who love to fish to throw in a line.

Because the high-elevation lakes do not naturally have any fish, amphibians previously dominated the waterways. As the bridge between water and land-based animals, amphibians begin life in fresh water as water-breathing larvae or tadpoles with gills, which they discard to begin life on land as air-breathing creatures. A primitive species, the Mount Lyell salamander resembles a lizard in shape, but its skin does not have scales. It lives in moist, sheltered areas, such as among the leaf litter on forest floors or near waterways. They are hard to find and are more readily seen in mating season in early spring at night in small pools. Frogs and toads—amphibians with tough skin—have powerful hind legs for jumping, well-developed ears, and large discs behind each eye. Yosemite toads, Pacific treefrogs, and several species of the endangered mountain yellow-legged frog

Garter snake swallowing a trout

Camouflaged white-tailed ptarmigan

live around the high lakes and streams. You may hear frogs from time to time, but if you are lucky enough to see one, leave it alone as some species are only slowly recovering from endangered status.

You may also encounter various small reptiles. Lizards are numerous, but because they are small and move quickly, you will likely have trouble identifying them. More recognizable, with its thin brown body with dark spots and long yellow stripes, is the western terrestrial garter snake, common around tree line. Because they are diurnal, you'll spot them near waterways, in grasslands, and even in small trees. They can grow to about three feet long and are harmless to humans.

If you're a bird-watcher, it's worth the weight to pack a small pair of binoculars because most of the birds in the High Sierra are summer visitors. Some that breed at lower elevations and visit tree line occasionally include swifts, hummingbirds, pigeons, kingfishers, flycatchers, swallows, nutcrackers, robins, and thrushes. Only a few birds breed above tree line. The gray-crowned rosy finch breeds in cliffs and outcrops but its dull gray to brown colors belie its name; look for its gray crown and pink highlights. The white-tailed ptarmigan is the only North American bird to spend its entire life cycle above tree line. About the size of a small chicken, it changes color according to the season. In summer the plumage is a mix of grays and browns, which renders it nearly impossible to see among rocks and grasses. In winter the feathers change to all white and its feathered feet allow it to walk on snow. You may encounter them close to trails, and they may not fly off but instead will sit quietly relying on their camouflage. If you encounter any, try not to disturb them—just tiptoe on by. In the skies, golden eagles soar above the peaks and meadows. These eagles are a fully protected species in California; while open grasslands are their preferred habit for hunting, you may see them in the summer in the Sierra, either singly or in pairs.

Keep your eye out for small mammals such as shrews and moles, which create shallow tunnels in meadows or stream banks. They eat insects and amphibians but are difficult to spot. You're more likely to see rodents such as various species of mice, rats, chipmunks, and squirrels. You'll probably see them scurrying up

Marmot on the lookout on a boulder

Mule deer browsing

and down trees in the subalpine areas. Mule deer also inhabit the forests of the subalpine zone; if you see them and they see you, they are shy and will move away if they feel threatened.

Above tree line, you may spot yellow-bellied marmots sunning themselves on large boulders near their burrows. These medium-sized mammals are about two feet long with reddish-brown fur and a pale-yellow belly. Their whistles are often the first sign of their presence. You're less likely to catch a glimpse of a pika, a member of the rabbit family. Like the marmot, the pika also lives among boulders, but they store grass in hay piles under rocks for winter. Listen for an "eep" and watch for a small furry mammal with rounded ears and big whiskers. We were fortunate to see several pika on our first trip in the range so did not realize they were an uncommon sight. We could have spent hours watching these cute little furballs gathering grasses, and then with mouths full, scurrying under rocks to secrete their haul.

Bighorn sheep, with their distinctive curly horns, range on the highest slopes of the peaks. They have been endangered because of habitat loss, disease, and overhunting, but a conservation program has successfully expanded their range. Their main predator, mountain lions, grow up to eight feet long and feed on deer and large rodents. Mountain lions are mainly nocturnal and generally shy of humans, but if you see one, be wary because some people have been attacked. If you encounter one, do not run or make any sudden movements; back away slowly waving your arms above your head to appear larger and reduce the likelihood that the cat will attack.

Black bears, which also inhabit the Sierra Nevada, are misnamed: They vary in color from light brown through to black. Backpackers need to be aware of bears, their habits, and their behavior. They will eat almost anything they find, ranging from acorns, berries, and fruit to insects, fish, small mammals, and carrion. They are not interested in eating you but extremely interested in the food you carry. While black bears can be active during the day, they are mainly nocturnal and are more common in lower forests where food sources are richer than at high elevations. Population pressure and loss of habitat have encouraged some black bears to move into higher forests, and while it is not common to see a bear near or above tree line, they occasionally venture into this zone. Black bears have a great sense of smell but poor eyesight. They will sometimes stand up on their hind legs to get a better look at you. If you encounter a bear, keep a safe distance, do not look it in the eyes, talk quietly, and do not run; many charges are bluffs meant to scare you. Hold out your arms to appear as big as possible and move slowly away upwind if possible. If the bear charges, do not run. If it attacks, fight back.

Although the California state flag features a grizzly bear, the species was extirpated in California in the 1920s. Grizzly bears are larger than black bears and their fur, similar in color to black bears, has a grizzled appearance. They eat the same food as black bears plus actively hunt larger mammals and fish. Once widespread throughout California, grizzly bears were poisoned and hunted to the point of extinction, so you can at least be assured that if you do see a bear in the High Sierra, it will not be a grizzly.

Only some of the flora and wildlife of the Seirra Nevada have been described here. As an observant backpacker, you can expect to discover plenty more species during your journey along the range.

PREPARATION & PLANNING

From the first step onto the trail to the last step back onto pavement, preparation and planning are crucial to an extended backpack through the Sierra Nevada, an epic aspiration. You will reduce the risks inherent to traveling through this high-elevation terrain for days on end and improve your chances of having an enjoyable trip. Your first step to having a safe journey is not on the trail but to your computer to ensure your medical insurance is up to date. If you're a US citizen, having insurance in case of a medical emergency is essential. If you're coming from another country, purchase travel insurance that will cover all medical costs you may incur while you're in the US.

WHEN TO GO

The optimal period for hiking the Sierra Grand Traverse is, generally, late July through mid-September. However, conditions in the Sierra Nevada can vary significantly from year to year depending on the amount of winter snowfall. In a low snow year, most passes will be clear of snow by early July, while in a high snow year, patches of snow can remain until mid-August. Temperatures start dropping significantly around mid-September, and although in some years late September can still be a good time for hiking, some facilities, such as resorts and bus services, start closing in early September.

The snow depth on the summit of Mammoth Mountain, provided on the ski and bike resort's website (see Resources), will help you know how much snow to expect on the Sierra Grand Traverse. If 150 inches or more is reported at the

Heading to Lake 10,855 (Section 4)

Campsite near Ireland Lake (Section 1)

start of June on the Mammoth Mountain summit, expect snow bands to persist on some passes through most of the summer. The snow melts quickly, so 150 inches in early June will normally melt away to around 20 inches by the end of July. If less than 100 inches is reported at the start of June then almost all of the snow will have melted by late July. Of course every year is slightly different, but the above provides a general guide to what you might encounter.

Summer holidays can be extra busy. The Fourth of July is early for the season, but Labor Day, the first weekend of September, will definitely mean more boots on trails as people take advantage of the long weekend and the unofficial last blast of summer. Try to avoid that holiday weekend for bus trips and restocking food.

GETTING THERE

Whether you're traveling from other states or from other countries, the main gateways for the Sierra Nevada are the San Francisco (SFO) and Los Angeles (LAX) international airports. Trains and buses are available from SFO and LAX to Tuolumne Meadows and the town of Mammoth Lakes so you can start the traverse at the very beginning. A flight goes between LAX and Mammoth Lakes daily, but flights are often cancelled because of problems with wind shear at the small Mammoth Lakes airstrip. The most reliable alternative by air from SFO or LAX is to fly to Reno, then take a three-and-a-half-hour bus ride (Monday through

Friday) from the airport south to Mammoth Lakes. For some flights, connecting with the bus on the same day is not possible, but overnight accommodation in Reno is generally inexpensive. Bus service continues to Bishop and Lone Pine and can be used to return to Reno at the end of the Sierra Grand Traverse. Multiple flights go to Reno each day from many airports around the US, making it the most reliable and flexible option for access.

PUBLIC TRANSIT

During summer, the Eastern Sierra Transit Authority (ESTA) operates a bus service Monday through Friday from the Reno airport south to Mammoth Lakes. ESTA has several services on the same days from Mammoth Lakes to Bishop and Independence, as well as a return the same day from Lone Pine. We have used that service to deliver a food drop to Independence. ESTA also runs Bishop Creek Shuttle from Bishop to South Lake and Lake Sabrina (near North Lake) twice a day, every day, from around mid-June until early September. The Yosemite Area Regional Transportation System (YARTS) runs a daily bus service during summer from Mammoth Lakes over Tioga Pass to Tuolumne Meadows and on to Yosemite Valley.

The Lakes Basin Shuttle is free around the town of Mammoth Lakes and provides access to the Sierra Grand Traverse at Horseshoe Lake. In summer one of the free shuttles in Mammoth Lakes connects to Adventure Park. From there, another bus continues to Reds Meadow; that fare includes a park entrance fee. While some summer services are scheduled to operate from mid-June to early-September, snow can delay their start date and can also cause them to shut down early for the season, so study timetables on services' websites and call them before relying on a particular service.

The alternative is to use charter services for transport, and there are several licensed operators. Over time, charter operators can change and we recommend you search online for "Sierra charters east" to find current operators. For some access points, such as Onion Valley and Horseshoe Meadows, this is the only public transit option available. While charter operators often leave at the same time each day, they provide a service only if they have bookings. Book ahead and contact the operator a day or two before a charter to confirm the service and time because they may alter pickup times to assist multiple backpackers.

Access by Car

Paved roads run from multiple directions to US Highway 395 on the east side of the Sierra Nevada. From the West Coast, access is via either State Route (SR) 120

Split rock beside John Muir Trail (Section 3, Leg 4)

(called Tioga Road through Yosemite National Park) to Tuolumne Meadows or Tioga Pass or via SR 178 over the southern end of the range to Inyokern on US 395. From the east, Interstate 80 runs through Reno and I-15 through Las Vegas with I-40 just to the south.

Using private transport to get to the start and then be picked up from the end requires planning. All sections of the Sierra Grand Traverse are thru hikes and require two separate cars to arrange a shuttle. You must drive both cars to your ending point then return in one car to your starting point. Allow a full day to drive from Horseshoe Meadows to Tuolumne Meadows. If you know someone locally, you may be able to arrange for them to pick you up at the end and either drive you to Tuolumne Meadows or drop you on US 395 from where you can catch a bus back to the start. Do not park in areas at trailheads designated as day parking, and do not leave any food items, including empty food wrappers, in your car. Black bears have a powerful sense of smell and have been known to break into cars in the Sierra for the smallest bits of food-scented items. At this time, wilderness pass holders do not have to pay any fees or permits to park at trailheads at Tuolumne Meadows in Yosemite NP and the other five trailheads, all in Inyo National Forest.

Renting a car is possible but not a cheap option; most of the time your rental will sit unused at trailheads. Cars can no longer be rented in Bishop, so your options are cities such as Reno, Los Angeles, and San Francisco. While you can visit Yosemite Valley by bus from Tuolumne Meadows, if you have a car, you can visit any number of nearby destinations such as the desert in Death Valley, view limestone formations in Mono Lake, find bristlecones in the White Mountains east of the Sierra, or explore old buildings in the ghost town of Bodie.

ACCLIMATIZATION

The Sierra Grand Traverse starts at 8580 feet, and most of this route is above that elevation. The first few days at elevation are hard if you are not acclimatized to elevations above sea level. In the Sierra Nevada, some hikers get altitude sickness, also known as Acute Mountain Sickness (AMS). This serious medical condition can result in death swiftly if you stay at elevation. Acclimatize as much as possible before starting by spending some time at higher elevations.

To begin your acclimatization process, fly to Reno and stay overnight; Reno is at an elevation of 5000 feet and you can easily find fairly inexpensive accommodations. The next day, catch the bus to Mammoth Lakes, which is higher again at 8000 feet, making it an ideal place to start acclimatizing; we suggest spending at least two nights there buying and packing food, walking around town, and, if time permits, hiking on trails at nearby higher elevations. Depending on how you

Cataract Creek Pass from Knapsack Pass (Section 4)

organize your food supplies, you might need another day to deliver food drops to Bishop, South Lake, and Independence.

If you have prepared all your food before you start, you will not need to include additional resupply days, beyond the time you need to collect your food parcels. An advantage of preparing food in advance is that you don't need to obtain a new wilderness permit at each resupply point (see Permits & Wilderness Regulations below). Mammoth Lakes is a resort town and accommodation is not cheap. However, the only other choice is the nearby town of Bishop, which has less expensive accommodation, but its elevation of only 4200 feet is not high enough for hikers to acclimatize fully.

Leave Mammoth Lakes by catching a bus to Tuolumne Meadows, and if you've already prebooked a permit, start walking that day to Nelson Lake (see Section 1, Leg 1). If you need to get a walk-up permit, join the line to obtain a wilderness permit (see Permits & Wilderness Regulations below). The office is 0.7 mile east of the Tuolumne Meadows post office and opens at 11 AM. If the permit is for the next day, camp in the backpackers' camping area. Before arriving, ensure the campground is open and available for wilderness backpackers since the area was recently renovated. You can then spend the afternoon hiking to Lembert Dome for excellent views of your surroundings.

Above tree line south of Bench Lake (Section 4)

SAFETY

When you backpack in the High Sierra, you are generally a considerable distance from medical assistance. Keep safety foremost in your mind as you undertake the traverse. While you can take many precautions to improve your safety, various aspects of backpacking in the high mountains, however, are not under your control. During summer, the Sierra Nevada often experiences long periods of mild weather, ideal walking conditions. However, every summer also has periods of poor weather, from several days of rain or a prolonged period with afternoon thunderstorms. When such storms are forecast, start early in the day and cross any high points as early as possible. Lightning strikes are a real danger in the range.

Before you depart on your trip, leave detailed information about yourself or your group and your proposed route and expected date of return with someone you trust and remember to notify them on return. If you have not contacted that person by your expected exit date, they are responsible for forwarding details about you and/or your group to emergency services to initiate a search. Do not rely on the rangers who collect your information and issue you a wilderness permit to initiate a search and rescue operation. They have no way of knowing when you depart the range, although if you have parked a car at a trailhead that is registered on your permit, it can serve as one clue that you are overdue.

While smartphones will work in a few places in the mountains, they cannot be relied on. Satellite phones are an expensive alternative that work with a clear view of the sky. The simplest system, an emergency position indicating radio beacon (EPIRB) or a satellite personal tracker (SPOT), signals authorities, using the GPS satellite system, that you are experiencing an emergency and need evacuation. New devices, such as Garmin's InReach, can be used to request an evacuation; it also sends and receives messages, which ensures your call has been received and the rescue body understands the urgency and required resources. Note that emergency requests should be used only for life-threatening events, not for mundane problems such as blisters or minor injuries that can be overcome by a day or two of rest.

Acute Mountain Sickness

When it happens, acute mountain sickness (AMS) can be a serious medical condition and can develop into HACE, high-altitude cerebral edema, or HAPE, high-altitude pulmonary edema. Since the bulk of the traverse is between 9500 and 12,000 feet, it is at a high enough elevation to cause AMS. If you develop AMS, the *only* solution is to descend to lower altitudes. Because of the remote location of much of the Sierra Grand Traverse, it is not always easy to descend. If you acclimatize before you start backpacking, you will vastly improve your chances of staying healthy and having a successful hike at altitude.

A NOTE ABOUT SAFETY

Safety is an important concern in all outdoor activities. No guidebook can alert you to every hazard or anticipate the limitations of every reader. Therefore, the descriptions of roads, trails, routes, and natural features in this book are not representations that a particular place or excursion will be safe for your party. When you follow any of the routes described in this book, you assume responsibility for your own safety. Under normal conditions, such excursions require the usual attention to traffic, road and trail conditions, weather, terrain, the capabilities of your party, and other factors. Keeping informed on current conditions and exercising common sense are the keys to a safe, enjoyable outing.

—*Mountaineers Books*

Water

The Sierra Nevada is blessed with a multitude of lakes. Even in a dry year, you can find water. The exception is when crossing passes: Be sure to carry sufficient water to tide you over until you get to the next lake. While most water sources look clean, they may contain contaminants harmful to people. The protozoa *Giardia lamblia*, carried in the feces of humans and animals, is a common water contaminant. Symptoms of infection are diarrhea, excessive gas, and muscle cramps. The parasite *Cryptosporidium* can also be found in mountain waters. Symptoms include diarrhea. Medical treatments are available for the conditions caused by these contaminants, but avoiding exposure to them is the better option.

The simplest, most effective way to treat water is to boil it for around five minutes. Boiling kills all organisms but consumes a lot of stove fuel, plus you have to wait for the water to cool. Chemical treatment is simple. Just add the specified dose to a measured quantity of water and wait until it is sterilized; cold water takes longer. Iodine is a common chemical treatment but is not effective against *Cryptosporidium*. Chlorine is more effective but adds an undesirable taste to water. Some chemical treatments are a mix of both chemicals but are trickier

Sunset at Golden Bear Lake (Section 5)

to use. Many backpackers use a water filter. Though fairly large and heavy when compared to chemical treatments or boiling, they are effective against most contaminants except viruses, which are rare. They work by pumping water through a very fine filter that allows water molecules to pass but stops larger particles. Devices that emit UV rays are light and effective for killing all organisms as long as the water is clear, but they are powered by batteries, and some are fragile and prone to breaking.

General Hygiene

In areas without a privy or toilet, select a site at least 100 feet away from all campsites and water sources, dig a hole at least six inches deep, and most importantly, cover it with soil when finished. Carry a small trowel for this purpose.

Wash all cooking gear well away from streams to prevent food scraps from polluting the water. Do not use soap, even biodegradable types. For dishwashing, a scourer or sand are just as effective and are pollution free.

ZERO DAYS

In the world of backpacking and thru hiking, a zero day means a day off from hiking to resupply, wash clothes, and run errands in a nearby town, or simply to rest.

Accounts that you may read online that indicate a twenty-day hike, for example, may actually mean twenty-six days in total. Such a timeframe would likely include several zero days spent walking out to a trailhead, getting resupplies in a town, and returning to the route. On hikes longer than a week, where hikers will need to resupply, the trip plan often includes some zero days.

ESTIMATING YOUR HIKING TIME

The estimates in the hiking timetable (below) assume that hikers live at sea level and will need to acclimatize to higher elevations and their corresponding lower levels of oxygen at the start. Because different hikers have different aims, we offer three suggestions: short, medium, and long. At the end of each of the five hiking sections, our suggestions assume hikers will walk to the road, catch a bus or shuttle into town to collect food parcels, stay overnight, and return by bus the next morning to continue hiking. We do not include any zero days between sections. There is no best or preferred number of days since it depends on how many hours you hike each day and what type of adventure you're seeking. In addition to the times supplied in the table, allow for one day at the end to get back to Mammoth Lakes by charter or bus and another day to return to Reno, San Francisco, Los Angeles, or other destinations.

The times in the table are for experienced, cross-country backpackers and do not include long stops, meal stops, and side trips. These estimates are based on

TABLE: HIKING TIME

TRAIL SECTION	SHORT (5–6 hours)	MEDIUM (7–8 hours)	LONG (9–10 hours)
Tuolumne to Horseshoe Lake	10	7	5
Horseshoe Lake to Piute Pass	10	7	5
Piute Pass to Lower Dusy Basin	4	4	3
Lower Dusy Basin to Kearsarge Lakes	8	6	4
Kearsarge Lakes to Horseshoe Meadows	7	5	4
TOTAL	39	29	21

Note: All values shown in table are hiking days. After you add 6 days to each total for acclimatizing, resupplying, and resting, the full trip could range from 27 days to as long as 45.

Blooming shooting stars near White Rock Saddle (Section 4)

our experience; use them to help you plan your trip. Some hikers may set a goal of finishing the traverse in a target time and so may move quickly, while others might like to savor the wildflowers or drink in extraordinary views from high passes. Your journey time will also depend on the snow cover and your exact route climbing and descending sections of scree. As you establish a rhythm in the early part of the traverse, you can adjust your expectations for the rest of your trip.

TIPS FOR CROSS-COUNTRY TRAVEL

Traveling cross-country in the Sierra requires hikers to consider the class ratings of passes, as well as effective techniques for hiking across scree. All the passes on the Sierra Grand Traverse are graded class 2. The only class 3 moves are a climb onto a six-foot-high ledge near North Glacier Pass (Section 1, Leg 5) and a short climb to a step onto a sloping granite slab near Dumbbell Pass (Section 4, Leg 3). Confident backpackers should have little trouble at these two places. Class 2 is defined as difficult cross-country travel where the use of

Climbing a rock slab beside Lake 11,540 (Section 3)

hands is required only for balance, such as on loose scree or steep gravel slopes. Class 3 requires the use of hands to climb up or down a rock face. Depending on snow conditions and the route you choose, you might need to make some class 3 moves on class 2 passes.

Most passes contain wide bands of scree: loose rock that has been shattered and moved by ice or snow. Most of the scree is stable—the entire slope does not start moving when a hiker stands or walks on it. Some individual stones are loose, so where possible, stepping between stones is generally safer. Scree is not difficult to climb or descend, but doing so safely takes time. You will also encounter a couple of steep, loose gravel slopes that you will need to descend. Zigzag down to reduce the angle of the slope. Ensure all group members cross in the same direction before turning so that if a rock or stone starts tumbling, it falls away from rather than onto hikers.

Traveling the entire traverse north to south has an advantage when it comes to passes without trails. The north side of Sierra passes are on the shady side of the range and have experienced more recent glaciation, meaning that they tend to be steeper and have more scree. Climbing, rather then descending, the steepest side of passes is easier because you can choose your route on the approach. While descending steep slopes seems easier than climbing them, in practice it is often difficult to select the easiest descent route because you cannot see the terrain below. In general, the southern side of passes are less steep, and as a result, routefinding when descending is usually easier.

Planning your route on the approach to a pass can save a lot of time and effort. Generally, select a route with the smallest scree or rocks and that avoids cliffs. Sometimes zigzagging, or switchbacking, as you go might take a little longer but can be easier if you follow grassy leads—strips of grass that grow as a result of stones or gravel having broken down enough to form soil—or smaller stones.

Minimum Impact Walking

All backpackers should aim to leave no trace of their visit (see the "Follow Leave No Trace Principles" sidebar). Select campsites on rock slabs or sandy or gravel terraces away from water. Fan out rather than walk in single file when the terrain allows. Do not erect ducks (small piles of rocks) or cairns to mark the route. Such markers are not needed on the Sierra Grand Traverse since most of the time the route is obvious. Moving stones and creating random cairns disrupts the natural ecosystem, works against the Leave No Trace Principles,

FOLLOW LEAVE NO TRACE PRINCIPLES

The nonprofit Leave No Trace (LNT) organization established the LNT principles as a framework of minimum-impact practices to apply in a variety of circumstances, but when adhered to in remote wilderness and areas such as the High Sierra, they can make a significant difference in keeping such places wild with minimum human impact. The LNT organization continually evaluates and reshapes the principles based on insights from scientists, land managers, and outdoor education leaders. Learn more at lnt.org. Here are the seven principles:

1. Plan ahead and prepare.
2. Travel and camp on durable surfaces.
3. Dispose of waste properly.
4. Leave what you find.
5. Minimize campfire impacts.
6. Respect wildlife.
7. Be considerate of others.

Campsite north of Merriam Lake (Section 2)

and, if cairns are oddly placed, encourages hikers to walk to the cairn location, potentially creating new trails.

Choosing a Campsite

Wilderness permits require campsites to be at least 100 feet (about 40 paces) from water sources. The exception is for established campsites or in very rocky areas where hikers can camp as close as 25 feet to water. Rules vary for each national park. To reduce damage, camp on sandy or hard surfaces and not on the fragile vegetation that flourishes in some meadows. Some lakes have suitable areas for camping, while at others, you may have a challenge finding good sites away from water. To help you in some instances, in the hike section of this guide, we've marked lakes that have flat areas at least 100 feet from water.

We encourage hikers to stay in areas where campsite damage and water pollution can be kept to a minimum. If you know which places have suitable areas for camping away from water sources, that will help you decide whether to camp where you are or continue on. Adhering to several Leave No Trace principles when camping (see sidebar, "Follow Leave No Trace Principles") minimizes the impact hikers have on these natural areas, ensuring that the next generation can experience the Sierra Nevada in a similar condition.

PERMITS & WILDERNESS REGULATIONS

Wilderness permits are compulsory for all overnight and longer trips in the Sierra Nevada, but they are not expensive. Of the daily quota available for each trailhead, 60 percent can be reserved 24 weeks (168 days) ahead of time. The remainder, called walk-up permits, are available on a first-come, first-served basis. Because the Sierra Grand Traverse starts at Tuolumne Meadows in Yosemite National Park, if you need a walk-up permit, join the queue at the wilderness permit office the day before you need it. The office, which opens at 11 AM, is 0.7 mile east of the Tuolumne Meadows post office. Be alert to possible changes in the permit allocation process. In 2020, for example, due to the pandemic, all permits were issued via online bookings only. See nps.gov/yose for current permit allocations.

The Tuolumne Meadows Campground may be closed for several years for a major upgrade, part of which involves moving the camping area for backpackers to the John Muir Trail trailhead. While it is being renovated, you cannot camp there overnight before starting the Sierra Grand Traverse. Instead, you must start walking on the day you collect your permit. For more information about the national park and this campground's status, visit nps.gov/yose.

To book a permit, you need to supply the following: entry and exit dates; entry and exit trails; total number in group, including the leader; group leader's name, address, and phone number; and proposed campsites during the trip. The permit system provides a fixed list of possible campsites. Most campsites on the Sierra Grand Traverse are not listed, so choose the nearest listed campsite. If booking online, study the list ahead of time so you can fill in the form quickly. The online booking system is timed and works best if you prepare all the details in advance. Note that you do not have to strictly follow your proposed itinerary—changes, due to weather, fitness, and other unforeseen events, are allowed.

A wilderness permit applies to continuous travel. You can descend to a road, collect a resupply, and ascend the next morning, but if you take more than twenty-four hours (a full zero day), then you must obtain a new permit that starts from the return point. If you plan to take zero days in towns, reserve all your permits in advance. If you plan to take a day off in Mammoth Lakes, for example, you will need to obtain a new permit from the Inyo National Forest Office in Mammoth Lakes for a Deer Lakes entry point. The reservation system is slightly different for Inyo National Forest because reservations open six months ahead of time as opposed to twenty-four weeks for Yosemite National Park.

You must carry your permit at all times in case a ranger asks to see it. If you cannot produce a permit when a ranger asks for it, you may be removed from the

Lake 11,910 from approach to Alpine Col (Section 3)

range and incur heavy fines. A permit can be used only for the designated entry point because there are daily quotas for each trailhead. But once permit holders have entered the Sierra Nevada, they can cross into any national park or national forest in the range. The rules differ slightly in each national park or forest; for example, campfires are banned above different elevations, depending on the managing agency and local restrictions. As most of the Sierra Grand Traverse is above tree line, you should not plan to have campfires anyway.

For this traverse, book a permit for "Nelson Lakes (cross-country)." If a Nelson Lakes permit is unavailable, a Rafferty Creek permit is an alternative that allows hikers to connect to the traverse around the 10-mile mark. Another alternative is to secure a permit from Inyo National Forest to start at Saddlebag Lake and follow the Sierra High Route southwest for two days to Tuolumne Meadows, where you can begin the traverse.

If you plan to use a fuel-based stove or light a fire (where permitted), you must also carry a valid California Campfire Permit. This free permit is available from Ready for Wildfire (see Resources). There is a link to the application on the same website where you book wilderness permits. The process is simple: Watch a video, pass a short quiz, then print out the permit. It is valid for one year.

Some regulations apply for the Sierra Grand Traverse regardless of your entry point. Bear canisters, for example, must be carried, and all food, toiletries, and garbage must be stored in them. They are bulky—and not light—but are effective at stopping bears from stealing backpackers' food and from becoming "problem" bears that land managers have to relocate or otherwise deal with. There is no alternative method for storing food safely from bears since most of the route is above tree line. While it is rare to encounter a bear, they are around (see more about bears earlier in this section). Other regulations—the requirement to always carry your permit, not to have fires above tree line, and that campsites should be away from water sources—are covered in detail above.

MAPS

This guide provides detailed topographic maps of the Sierra Grand Traverse. The maps display the NAD 83 grid and can be used in conjunction with a GPS receiver or app. Set the GPS unit to UTM and a NAD 83 grid instead of the default degrees, minutes, and seconds. Grid numbers are shown around the edges of each

Dumbbell Lakes (Section 4)

map in this book. To convert the full UTM grid displayed on a GPS unit, for both eastings and northings, ignore the last three digits. The next two digits are the grid numbers on the book maps. Use the next digit that was initially ignored to interpolate where you are located within a grid square.

While the maps in this book show the general route, they do not depict the greater area or all access trails. If you must retreat, other maps are essential. The Tom Harrison series has the best overall maps for backpackers. These maps have a 1:80,000 scale, and the detail on adjacent maps is consistent. They show all hiking trails, making them essential for trips in the range.

For more detail, obtain the US Geological Survey (USGS) 7.5-minute topographic series, which have a scale of 1:24,000 and show vegetation, glaciers, and semi-permanent snowfields. While they are very detailed, the series is inconsistent with adjacent maps, which show varying levels of detail. Most trails are not shown on these maps, making them problematic for backpackers. While useful for a detailed picture of the terrain, the lack of trail data reduces their value. They can be downloaded for free from usgs.gov.

GEAR & SUPPLIES

All backpackers venturing into the High Sierra must be self-sufficient. It is essential to have reliable equipment in working order. Gear lists vary for each individual and evolve through experience. For those with less experience, the following list is a guideline for a summer trek of Sierra Grand Traverse.

Personal Equipment to Carry or Wear

These items encompass what you carry or wear, including supplies required for side trips.

Boots or trail runners: Your shoes must be comfortable and provide suitable support. If you wear trail runners, which wear out more easily, carry a spare pair or put a pair in your resupply box.

Compass and GPS unit or app: Each member should carry a reliable means to navigate and know how to use it.

First-aid kit: Pack what you need for minor injuries and ailments.

Hats: Beanie or balaclava for warmth (preferably wool or fleece); shade hat for sun protection

High-energy food: Dried fruit, chocolate, and sweets for for an energy boost

Insect headnet: You will be glad to have one when insects are swarming.

THE TEN ESSENTIALS

This handy list of essential gear was originally developed by The Mountaineers.

1. **Navigation (map and compass):** Carry a topographic map of the area and know how to read it. A compass or GPS unit is also useful.
2. **Sun protection (sunglasses and sunscreen):** Even on wet days, carry sunscreen and sunglasses; you never know when the clouds will lift. At higher elevations your exposure to UV rays is much more intense than at sea level. You can easily burn on snow and near water.
3. **Insulation (extra clothing):** Carry raingear, wind-resistant layers, and insulating layers as well.
4. **Illumination (flashlight/headlamp):** Carry extra batteries too.
5. **First-aid supplies:** At the very least your kit should include bandages, gauze, scissors, tape, tweezers, pain relievers, antiseptics, and perhaps a small manual. Consider first-aid training through a program such as MOFA (Mountaineering Oriented First Aid).
6. **Fire (firestarter and matches):** Be sure you keep your matches dry. Resealable plastic bags do the trick.
7. **Repair kit and tools:** A knife is helpful; a multitool is better. A basic repair kit should include such things as nylon cord, a small roll of duct tape, some 1-inch webbing and extra webbing buckles (to fix broken pack straps), and a small tube of superglue. Safety pins can work wonders too.
8. **Nutrition (extra food):** Always pack more food than you need. Bring energy bars for emergency pick-me-ups.
9. **Hydration (extra water):** Carry two full water bottles, unless you will be hiking entirely along a water source. Carry a method for treating water.
10. **Emergency shelter:** This item can be as simple as a garbage bag, or something more efficient such as a reflective space blanket. A poncho can double as an emergency tarp.

Jacket: Must have a hood and be waterproof and windproof
Maps and guidebook: Keep in plastic bags.
Mittens or gloves: Socks can serve as a substitute.
Rain pants: Must be waterproof and fit over all clothing

The gully above Lake Ursa (Section 2)

Insulating shirt or sweater: Warm long-sleeve fleece, shirt, or sweater; layer up for insulation

Pants and shorts: Loose fitting

Socks: Wool or wool blend

Sunscreen: Essential, especially when above tree line

Pocketknife: Multipurpose device

Water bottle: Essential during the day while on the trail

Whistle: Carry at all times.

Personal Equipment for Your Pack

You'll also want to have the following items stowed in your backpack.

Batteries: Carry spares and a method for recharging them.

Bear canister: Compulsory for storing all food, toiletries, and garbage

Camera: Optional; use plastic bag or dry bag to keep dry.

Flashlight: Carry spare batteries.

Food: Bring all that you need for the trip, plus a one-day emergency reserve.

Sleeping bag liner: Keeps your bag clean and adds warmth

Light trail runners or sandals: Optional; use as spare footwear and around camp.

Nylon cord: For tying tents to rocks, as spare laces, clothesline, and other emergency uses

Pack: Must be durable and large enough to carry everything.

Sleeping bag: Temperatures can fall below freezing; a quality bag is essential.

Sleeping mat: Solid foam or inflating

Spare clothing: A change of clothing that you keep dry

Socks: Carry several pairs of wool or wool blend.

Toiletries: Small towel, toothbrush, toilet paper, and other personal essentials

Utensils: Mug, bowl, knife, fork, and spoon

TIPS FOR LIGHTENING YOUR LOAD

Take some simple steps when evaluating your gear and supplies and packing it to lighten your load and keep your pack nice and compact.

- Use travel containers that are small and will help you limit the amounts you carry to what you need.
- If you need to use stuff sacks and pouches, ensure they are made from lightweight materials.
- Reduce your first-aid kit to the essentials and those items frequently used.
- Ensure most items have several uses. A length of cord can replace a broken shoelace or be a tent guyline, clothes can become your pillow, and meal pouches can become garbage bags.
- Minimize clothing. Wear one set for hiking, and carry another set for sleeping or to wear when washing hiking clothes.
- Saving a little weight, but much space, make your second water bottle a collapsible one.
- Repacking meals from foil pouches into zippered plastic bags saves a little weight and makes packing bear canisters much easier.
- Carry a tent made from the lightest materials. Such tents are usually more expensive but can weigh significantly less.

Group Equipment

These items include equipment that a hiking party can share and divvy up among their packs as they wish.

Bottles or water bladder: Handy for carrying water to camp

Cooking kit: Pots as needed for the group

First-aid kit: At least one group member should know how to use contents.

Fuel: Labeled, leak-proof bottle or gas canisters

Insect repellent: Helps to keep mosquitoes, biting flies, etc. away when you are cooking and eating

Pot scrubber: Do not use dish soap.

Emergency communications device: To signal rescue services in a life-threatening emergency; satellite phone, SPOT, or InReach are options.

Stove: Essential for cooking; fires are banned above tree line.

Tent or tent fly: Essential for rain; double-skin tents are recommended to keep out mosquitoes.

Trowel: For burying feces

Water treatment: Carry some method for treating water for drinking.

The Miter from Miter Basin (Section 5)

FOOD LOGISTICS

Because most hikers travel from elsewhere to walk the Grand Traverse, they will have to decide on a resupply strategy. You can either bring most of your food, bring some of it and purchase the rest locally, or purchase all of it locally. If you are traveling to the Sierra from within the US, you can bring all your food for the trip. International travelers are banned from bringing several food items into the US, including meat, milk products, and some vegetables and fruit. If you intend to bring food, check with the US customs website (cbp.gov) since import rules can change.

Two outdoor retailers in Mammoth Lakes stock a wide range of freeze-dried meals. Vons, a medium-sized supermarket, and several other shops and outlets sell some food items suitable for hiking. If pre-packed freeze-dried meals satisfy, then enough items are available in town. If you seek more variety or like to create your own meals, you can order some food direct from manufacturers and have it posted or freighted to a hotel or other accommodation where you are booked. Check with the place you plan to stay first to see if they will accept parcels. An alternative is to have parcels posted to: Your Name, General Delivery, Mammoth Lakes Post Office, Mammoth Lakes, CA 93546.

To ensure delivery, place orders around two weeks before your arrival. Note that freeze-dried vegetables are not an ideal option due to their bulk; dehydrated vegetables are a more compact option.

Resupplying Food & Fuel

Hikers have four possible resupply points to choose from: Mammoth Lakes, North Lake, South Lake, and Onion Valley. Other possible resupply points are all a longer walk from the Sierra Grand Traverse. The most expensive but time-saving option is to have a food resupply brought up to the top of the range by horses from a pack station. It will save a long descent and ascent that may require one or two days walking each way. Pack stations offer this service near most of the trailheads. If you opt to resupply this way, arrive at the agreed-upon point early, then be patient and wait. Pack stations can run late for a wide variety of reasons, including difficulty rounding up and saddling horses, ice on the trail, or a horse coming up lame.

Two other options are to deliver food parcels to places on or near the trail that typically store them for backpackers or to mail food to General Delivery at the closest post office. If using general delivery, include an ETA date after your name to reduce the risk of the post office returning your parcel early. Note that stove fuel cannot be shipped through the US Postal Service. Places that will store food parcels typically charge a fee. Red's Meadow Resort, which is on the route, accepts food parcels. Near South Lake, Parchers Resort will store a food parcel. There are no other accommodations close to the Sierra Grand Traverse. For the North Lake access, leave food in Bishop or resupply in town. Bishop has supermarkets and outdoor retailers that sell freeze-dried meals. For Onion Valley access, leave food in Independence. This small town has only two small shops attached to gas stations, good for snacks and beef jerky, but very limited for meals.

Do not place food parcels in bear boxes at the end of the road for extended periods. Bear boxes beside parking lots are provided for day hikers to temporarily store food because bears sometimes destroy cars to get at food left in them. Don't be tempted by these boxes; rangers check the bear boxes regularly and clean them out.

A common method for resupply is to take a shuttle or charter bus into the nearest town, stay overnight, collect the resupply parcel, and return the next morning. Post offices are generally open between 9 AM and 5 PM Monday through Friday and on Saturday from 9 AM to noon. A summer bus runs from Lake Sabrina (a short walk from North Lake) and South Lake into Bishop. Onion Valley does not have any scheduled services. Charter services can be booked from Onion Valley to Independence. The Mt. Williamson Motel in Independence offers a package: For a fixed price, they organize transport to and from Onion Valley, provide overnight accommodation and breakfast, store a food parcel, and do one load of wash.

If exiting to a parking lot to meet charter transport, contact the operator the day before if possible to confirm details since some exit points have multiple parking lots and trailheads. Arrive early since most operators cannot wait long. If you expect to be late, contact the operator early to make alternative arrangements.

Food Storage

The best method for preventing bears from stealing food is to use bear canisters. Bears can weigh up to five hundred pounds, so canisters must be strong; you can find a variety of approved models with a quick online search. For most of the Sierra Grand Traverse, backpackers are required to carry and use approved bear canisters for all food and other scented items such as toothpaste. While the canisters are not light and figuring out how to situate them in your pack can be challenging, after a few days you'll establish a packing method.

Bear canisters can be rented, but for trips longer than a few weeks, buying them is a better option. Rental canisters are usually heavier and often smaller

Wright Creek backdropped by not-so-distant craggy peaks (Section 5)

than some of the popular models you can buy. The most cost-effective ones are made from strong plastic and weigh about two pounds. Locking mechanisms vary from model to model, but what they have in common is that a bear paw cannot open the lids. The lightest canisters are made from carbon fiber but are expensive and have sharp edges that, with frequent use, can wear holes in packs, unlike the rounded edges on plastic ones. As an estimate, one day's food for one person requires about 100 cubic inches, about 1.6 liters, of volume. Large bear canisters range in size from 600 to 700 cubic inches and can hold up to seven days of food for one person.

Bears are smart and many are familiar with canisters, especially in popular parks and along busy trails in the Sierra. They might examine it briefly to see if the lid is secured but will generally lose interest if they can't open it. If a bear does get into your food, do not try to retrieve it because the bear will defend the prize it has won. Accept the fact, clean up the mess after the bear has left, and hike out to the nearest resupply point.

For a side trip, remove the canister from your pack and store it in nearby rocks. Do not store canisters close to cliff edges because some bears have been

Climbing suncups to Russell Pass (Section 1)

known to roll them over the edge and break them. Similarly, do not store them beside rivers or lakes. Canisters are round in part because it makes it difficult for bears to carry them, so do not add ropes or ties. The canisters are also effective at keeping out other animals such as marmots and chipmunks. If you leave your pack behind while taking a side trip, empty it and open all the pockets so that a bear will not rip it apart looking for anything edible. We find it's better to not take any risk of a passing bear pawing through our belongings, so we carry our almost empty backpacks with our spare clothing, water, and snacks on any side trips.

In camp, prepare and eat food well away from tents. Never store any food, toothpaste, or strongly scented items in a tent when sleeping. When you are using a canister, keep the lid on. While hikers are allowed to hang food in trees in some areas of the Sierra Nevada, it is difficult to do so along the Sierra Grand Traverse since most of it is above tree line.

EQUIPMENT FOR SNOW TRAVEL

In a high snow year, hikers will almost certainly encounter bands of snow on some passes. Backpackers will need to figure out their strategy for walking safely on snow ahead of time. Microspikes have short, crampon-like spikes connected by links with an upper elastic cage that stretches over boots or trail runners. They are relatively light, make snow travel easier and safer, come in several sizes, and are adjustable to fit most footwear. They work well on compacted or semi-frozen snow and can save you from having to undertake a long bypass around bands of sloping snow.

On steep snow slopes where microspikes are insufficient, you may need to cut steps. In a high snow year, most hikers will find that carrying an ice axe for cutting steps is essential. While you may use it in only a few places, it will make traveling up steep snow slopes much easier—you'll be glad you brought it.

CAMPSTOVES

Fires are banned above tree line in all national parks and wilderness areas in the Sierra Nevada. As the Sierra Grand Traverse is mostly above tree line, plan to carry enough fuel for all your cooking needs. Compressed isobutane gas is the most popular backpacking fuel and the canisters are readily available. Fuel consumption varies from one person to another and is best worked out by experience on previous trips. If unsure, detailed calculators online can provide a starting point. Calculate your fuel needs, and then add a contingency factor of 10 percent. Slightly more is better than not quite enough!

HOW TO USE THIS GUIDE

This guidebook is designed for hikers with some cross-country experience who want to undertake an extended, cross-country hike in the Sierra Nevada. Experience following maps and navigating using landmarks are essential skills. While we have described the way through an area, following the easiest route requires at least some experience with cross-country travel in alpine areas. On the steeper passes, first-time cross-country hikers can expect to take longer than the suggested range of times.

Tackle the Sierra Grand Traverse in full or in sections. We've broken it into five sections that range from 26.5 to 48.8 miles long, which start and end near a major trail or trailhead. Many hikers use these access points as resupply locations. Each section is broken down further into legs, short segments bookended by easy-to-identify landmarks. Some of the trailheads are a considerable distance from the traverse. We've provided descriptions of trails to access points.

Each section begins with key data about the traverse. **Total distance** is the overall mileage as measured from maps. Because you will switchback in places to avoid big rocks, small lakes, and other obstacles, expect to walk a bit farther than the indicated mileage. No two hikers will follow exactly the same route. The **range of times** gives an overall estimate for that section. Trying to determine the number of hours walking by using a formula of overall distance and average walking speed does not work very well on this particular route. Conditions vary widely from well-maintained trails to steep scree-filled passes. While some people will walk faster and others slower, a rough indication of the time required is more useful for this type of walk than the overall distance.

Creek running into Thousand Island Lake (Section 1)

The jumbled terrain of Army Pass (Section 5)

On-trail and **off-trail** distances give totals of the type of terrain for that section. **Elevation gain and loss** (to the nearest 10 feet) is the cumulative total for the section; it gives you an idea of how much climbing and descending is involved. The key data also includes **low and high points, maps,** and crucial information in **permits and regulations.** We do not provide an itinerary as we don't want to promote overuse of any particular campsites. You'll find so many beautiful spots!

The **introduction** provides a summary of the route and what you can expect in that section. Next, you'll find descriptions of the **access** to the start and end of the section, which includes public transit if available. **Connecting trails,** from partway along the section, are next. Knowing about these trails is useful in case you need to leave partway along a section such as for illness, injury, weather conditions, or some other reason. You'll find a map of the entire section, indicating each leg, along with an elevation profile also indicating beginning and end points.

Leg descriptions, with a map and an elevation profile, are next. You'll also see a **cumulative elevation gain and loss** for each leg along with the total length of the leg in miles and a suggested range of hours that leg requires. The range does not include stops to rest, enjoy the view, or prepare and eat a meal. The legs start and end at a landmark, either a connecting trail or a suggested campsite, usually near a lake. The legs are not equal to a single day's walk; you can walk some in a few hours while others take more than one day.

Next comes the most useful part, the **detailed route description.** A summary of the leg gives an overview along with any special information. The detailed description then tells you how to follow the leg. Because most lakes and many of the high points are not named in the Sierra Nevada, it can sometimes be difficult to know exactly which point the walking notes are talking about. To help you know exactly where you are, look for the cumulative distance in miles at the appropriate point of each part of the route; for example: (**42.7**). This distance is also labeled beside the point of reference on the maps included in this guide. The route description provides directions and landmarks to aim for and gives general advice as to the best or easiest choice. Most of the time the description leaves it to you to decide precisely where to walk within broad parameters.

Sidebars cover alternative routes and side trips. The descriptions follow the same style as the rest of the leg and include the relevant distance marker both in the text, as above, and on the map so you can pinpoint your location as you follow the guide.

In this guide, **trail** indicates a maintained, obvious trail. An **unmarked trail** refers to a clearly defined but usually rougher trail that is not maintained by any of the park services. You may lose these trails in open or rocky areas since they are unofficial and therefore unmarked. A **use trail** describes a walking path that has formed through repeated use. Such trails are often well-defined where there is only one narrow route but often braid and fade out when the terrain opens up. A **route** describes a way without consistent trail that you must navigate carefully. If you're an experienced navigator, you should have few problems, since in many cases the next objective is obvious. If you plan to walk south to north, look for information for some of the more difficult locations at the end in *italic*.

The maps indicate suggested places to camp. These are not the only campsites, but rather places where we found either an established site or a fairly flat

MAP LEGEND

-------	Featured leg on trail	◭	Frontcountry campsite
---------	Featured leg off trail	▲	Suggested campsite
··············	Alternate route	⬯	Water
-·-·-·-·-·	Adjacent traverse leg	⌇	River or creek
----------	Other trails	☀	Swamp or marsh
————	Highway	⋇	Falls
————	Secondary road	▦	Glacial ice or snow
(395)	US highway	Ⓣ	Trailhead
(178)	State route	🚌	Bus stop
○	Town	▲	Peak or high point
⋈	Bridge	■	Point of interest
⌐---⌐	Boundary	12,140	Elevation in feet
	Forest	⌣	Pass or gap
no camping	Restriction	● 25.8	Mileage marker
⊕ (N)	True North	●	Start and end of leg

gravel, stony, or sandy bench at least 100 feet (40 paces) away from a water source. Some of the highest lakes are in steep bowls with small attractive flat areas beside them, but they are not appropriate for camping. We've seen evidence of others camping far too close to lakes on sensitive surfaces, so our campsite suggestions encourage you to make environmentally sound decisions when camping. In addition, being aware of potential campsite locations could help when you decide whether to stay or push on to the next water source where it may be difficult to find a campsite away from water.

YOUR ADVENTURE AWAITS

Having read the sections about climate, geology, fauna, and flora, you'll have a solid overview of what a traverse of the range offers. Then, having perused the preparation and planning notes, you'll know how to use this guide, how important it is to acclimatize, and all about other safety issues, environmental considerations, regulations, and necessary permits. It's time to plan your own trip, organize your resupplies and travel details, pack your pack, and begin your journey along the Sierra Grand Traverse.

This is your opportunity to experience a remote journey with off-trail sections in generally mild weather conditions compared to most other high-altitude mountain ranges. Magnificent sunrises and sunsets with glowing rock faces reflected in calm lakes are a definite highlight. You'll have almost daily views of craggy peaks and serrated ridges, pristine alpine lake basins, meadow-filled valleys, and an abundance of colorful wildflowers. Your adventure awaits in this spectacular range of light!

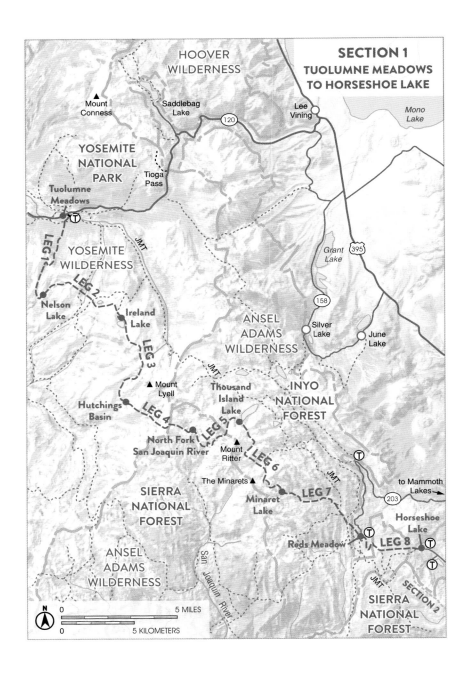

SECTION 1
TUOLUMNE MEADOWS
TO HORSESHOE LAKE

HOOVER
WILDERNESS

Mount
Conness

Saddlebag
Lake

120

Lee
Vining

Mono
Lake

YOSEMITE
NATIONAL
PARK

Tioga
Pass

Tuolumne
Meadows

T

LEG 1

YOSEMITE
WILDERNESS

JMT

395

Grant
Lake

LEG 2

Nelson
Lake

Ireland
Lake

158

ANSEL
ADAMS
WILDERNESS

Silver
Lake

June
Lake

LEG 3

JMT

Mount
Lyell

Thousand
Island
Lake

INYO
NATIONAL
FOREST

Hutchings
Basin

LEG 4

LEG 5

North Fork
San Joaquin River

Mount
Ritter

T

LEG 6

The Minarets

to Mammoth
Lakes

Minaret
Lake

LEG 7

JMT

203

SIERRA
NATIONAL
FOREST

Horseshoe
Lake

ANSEL
ADAMS
WILDERNESS

San
Joaquin
River

Reds Meadow

T

LEG 8

T

T

JMT

SECTION 2

SIERRA
NATIONAL
FOREST

N

0   5 MILES

0   5 KILOMETERS

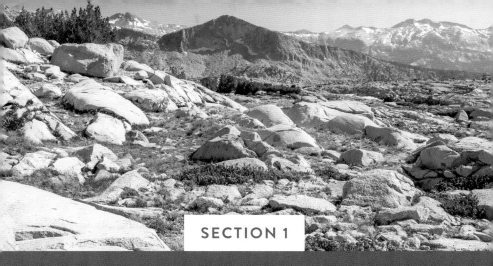

SECTION 1

TUOLUMNE MEADOWS
TO HORSESHOE LAKE

DISTANCE: 46.9 miles
TIME: 5 to 10 days
ON-TRAIL: 15.6 miles
OFF-TRAIL: 31.3 miles
ELEVATION GAIN: +13,830 feet
ELEVATION LOSS: -13,510 feet
LOW POINT: 7560 feet
HIGH POINT: 12,240 feet
MAPS: Harrison: Yosemite High Country,
Mammoth High Country; USGS: Tenaya
Lake, Vogelsang Peak, Mount Lyell,
Mount Ritter, Mammoth Mountain,
Crystal Crag

PERMITS & REGULATIONS

Obtain a wilderness permit from the
Wilderness Center at Tuolumne Meadows.

ABOVE: *Entering Hutchings Basin*

Camping is prohibited within 4 miles of
Tuolumne Meadows. Difficulty varies
according to snow conditions on Russell
Pass, one of the most challenging passes
on the Sierra Grand Traverse.

LEGS

1. Tuolumne Meadows to Nelson Lake
2. Nelson Lake to Ireland Lake
3. Ireland Lake to Hutchings Basin
4. Hutchings Basin to North Fork San
    Joaquin River
5. North Fork San Joaquin River to
    Thousand Island Lake
6. Thousand Island Lake to Minaret Lake
7. Minaret Lake to Reds Meadow
8. Reds Meadow to Horseshoe Lake

The Sierra Grand Traverse begins on a maintained trail to Elizabeth Lake. An unmarked trail then leads over a straightforward pass without any major challenges to scenic Nelson Lake. Tackle your first off-trail section with a climb to Reymann Lake then cross another uncomplicated pass and the valley of Rafferty Creek to reach the large, alpine lakes Evelyn and Ireland, both of which have wide, glacier-carved meadows.

The gentle off-trail hiking ends abruptly with some rugged pass crossings as the traverse enters the alpine zone dominated by rocky peaks, scree, and in some summers, snowfields. The Sierra Grand Traverse crosses four passes as it weaves south through the Cathedral Range. Between the passes, there are some pretty lake basins surrounded by rugged peaks. The traverse then joins the Sierra High Route (SHR) before crossing North Glacier Pass and follows along the side of the scenic Ritter Range to Minaret Lake. From Minaret Lake, you then follow maintained trails to the Devils Postpile and over Mammoth Pass to end the section at Horseshoe Lake near the town of Mammoth Lakes.

ACCESS

This section can be accessed from the north along Tioga Road in Yosemite National Park and on the south end via either Reds Meadow or Horseshoe Lake near Mammoth Lakes.

North: Tuolumne Meadows

Access Tuolumne Meadows via Tioga Road, a major paved road that crosses the entirety of Yosemite National Park. (It is California State Route 120 outside the park.) At Tuolumne Meadows, you'll find a campground with an area for

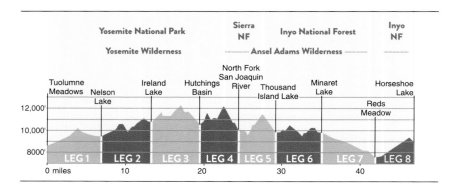

Lyell Fork Merced River Basin

backpackers, a post office that will store your food parcels for a fee, a grill that provides simple meals, and a small general store. The store sells basic hiking food and canisters of compressed gas, but do not rely on it for your entire resupply as items do sell out during busy periods. During summer the post office is open Monday through Friday and Saturday mornings. The grill is open 8 AM to 6 PM.

Facilities at Tuolumne Meadows are seasonal and usually open from late June until mid-September but can vary, depending on when Tioga Road closes as a result of snowfall. The Tuolumne Meadows Campground is closed temporarily for a major upgrade. For more information, visit nps.gov/yose.

South: Horseshoe Lake

Two access points are possible at the end of this section. The first, Reds Meadow, near the end of the section, has a resort and pack station. The resort, open in summer, has a café, cabins, and hot showers for a fee as well as a building to store hiker resupply packages. Fees apply for all resort services. A shuttle bus runs regularly in summer to the nearby town of Mammoth Lakes. Hikers must pay a national park fee to ride the bus.

For the other access point, follow the Sierra Grand Traverse to the end of this section by going over Mammoth Pass to Horseshoe Lake in Mammoth Lake Basin. A free shuttle bus, Lakes Basin Trolley, operates at about half-hour intervals from the basin into the nearby town of Mammoth Lakes. The bus operates from early July to late September (see Resources).

A reliable supply point, Mammoth Lakes has a resident population of about eight thousand with services such as restaurants, overnight accommodations, a supermarket, and several outdoor retailers. Some of the overnight places will store excess baggage, including resupply packages, for hikers who have a reservation. A ski resort in winter, Mammoth Lakes is a mountain biking and hiking destination in summer. Expect resort prices for some services.

Connecting Trails

If you need to retreat, the following list of shortest routes to services or a trailhead will be useful. Between Tuolumne Meadows and Ireland Lake (the end of Leg 2), the Sierra Grand Traverse crosses or meets several trails, which hikers could follow to retreat north to Tuolumne Meadows. From Maclure Lake (Leg 3), head northeast down Maclure Creek to the John Muir Trail (JMT) and follow it northwest to Tuolumne Meadows.

From Hutchings Basin and Lyell Fork Merced River (Leg 3), follow the streams downstream to the trail above the Merced River and continue on trails northward over Vogelsang Pass to Tuolumne Meadows, about a two-day walk. From Thousand Island Lake onward (Legs 5 to 8), head east to meet the JMT, then follow trails southeast to the closest road point at Agnew Meadows. The shuttle bus from Reds Meadow to Mammoth Lakes stops there.

1 TUOLUMNE MEADOWS TO NELSON LAKE

DISTANCE: 7.3 miles
ELEVATION GAIN/LOSS: +1850 feet / -820 feet
TIME: 3½–4½ hours

Initially on a maintained trail to Elizabeth Lake, the traverse then follows a use trail to Nelson Lake. Like many use trails, parts are very well defined, while in open areas and sparse forest, it can braid and fade out. Your journey begins (**0.0**) by looking for the trail to Elizabeth Lake at the south end of Tuolumne Meadows Campground.

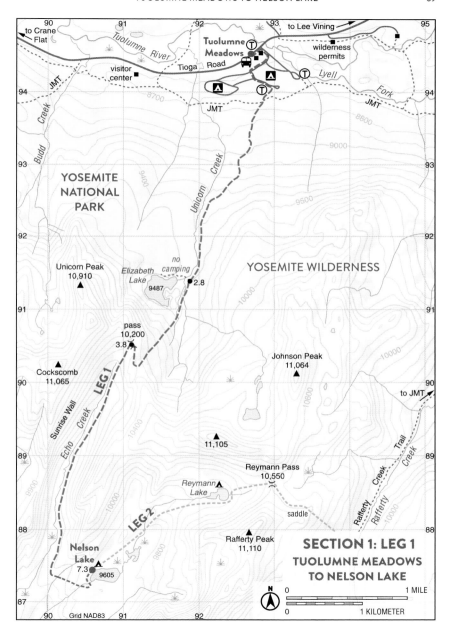

SECTION 1: LEG 1
TUOLUMNE MEADOWS
TO NELSON LAKE

Looking south from Echo Creek

From Tioga Road, follow the access road southeast into the campground. Turn right at the first two junctions, then turn left and pass the group camping area, and finally turn left again. The trail starts on the right just before the end of the road. From the backpackers camp, look for the trail at the top of the next road to the southwest. Follow the maintained hiking trail southward. At the time of writing, the campground was being renovated, so the start of the trail will likely change as a result. You soon cross the John Muir Trail, then climb gently to an unmarked trail junction beside Unicorn Creek, the outlet creek of Elizabeth Lake. The trail on the right crosses the outlet creek for a short side trip to the lakeshore, popular with day trippers. Note that camping is prohibited near the lake.

From the trail junction near Elizabeth Lake (**2.8**), follow the unmarked but well-used path south beside Unicorn Creek then across a meadow into forest. The use trail climbs steadily and becomes fainter and harder to follow as it rises

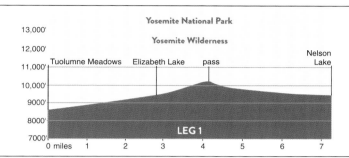

to the edge of the forest below bare rocky slopes. Follow the faint trail and climb a gully then swing right, heading northwest into the wide saddle, which at about 10,200 feet and beneath Unicorn Peak, is the first pass on the traverse (**3.8**).

Continue from the unnamed pass on a poorly defined use trail south-southwest and descend open gravel slopes into the valley of Echo Creek. The trail soon becomes better defined as it passes through open forest then runs along the eastern edge of a long meadow. About 3 miles from the pass, the trail swings left (east) and rises over a low ridge. You then descend on slabs into a small, forested gully. Be careful not to lose the use trail in this area. Cross the gully and climb briefly east and then north to the outlet of Nelson Lake. You'll find many fine campsites scattered around the lake.

2 NELSON LAKE TO IRELAND LAKE

DISTANCE: 5.6 miles
ELEVATION GAIN/LOSS: +2190 feet / -1060 feet
TIME: 5–6 hours

Your first off-trail challenge on this traverse is a climb to Reymann Lake. While not difficult, the climb includes rocky outcrops that may require short diversions. As you approach the lake, you'll see the outlet stream following multiple channels through many small ponds. You must choose which side of the creek to follow well before you reach the lake. From the lake, follow a rocky route east to Reymann Pass.

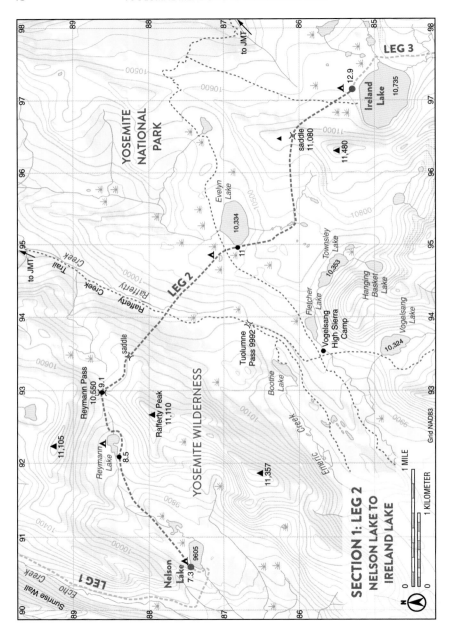

SECTION 1: LEG 2
NELSON LAKE TO
IRELAND LAKE

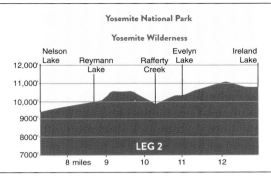

From the pass, the route becomes less rocky as you cross a deep valley to a wide meadow near Evelyn Lake. Continue traveling off-trail over a saddle to the large, grassy meadow beside Ireland Lake. While they no longer have any permanent ice, you can identify the lake's and meadow's glacial origins. The wide U-shaped valley is flanked by steep ridges and the retreating glacier left behind Ireland Lake with its steep headwall.

You can walk on either side of Nelson Lake (**7.3**) to reach its northern shore, but the trek along the west side is shorter. The unmarked trail ends here. For the rest of this leg, you will be choosing your way cross-country. From the north side of Nelson Lake, head northeast across an open meadow, passing west of a small lake; steer clear of marshy areas in this region. Continue northeast and cross the creek that flows into Nelson Lake, then climb steadily up the canyon. Numerous rocky outcrops provide views, some of which require short zigzagging detours, but the route remains straightforward. When the climb eases, veer gently to the right (east) up a series of slabs to Reymann Lake (**8.5**). The meadows around the lake are often wet, and the driest campsites are tucked among trees on the north side.

Follow either side of the lake to the inlet creek at the east end. Just north of the creek, climb steeply eastward into forest. The rocky bluffs are easier to scale than they may appear on first viewing them and preferable to fighting your way through the willows surrounding the creek. Once you are above the bluffs, traverse rocky slopes east to Reymann Pass (**9.1**).

From the pass, descend briefly southeast and traverse a boulder-strewn slope to a small saddle on the spur coming off Rafferty Peak. A short side trip to the knoll to the left (north) provides a fine view of the route ahead. Continue descending southeast as you pass through a section of sparse forest into the open valley of

Meadow near Nelson Lake

Rafferty Creek. Cross the maintained Rafferty Creek Trail to Tuolumne Pass, then climb steeply in untracked sparse forest to the open plateau above. Pass a small lake and then cross another trail to the southwest corner of Evelyn Lake. You will find there is scenic but exposed camping on patches of gravel on the open plateau.

From the southwest corner of Evelyn Lake (**11**), climb a short, steep stretch southeast that leads onto the broad spur above the lake. Follow this spur eastward to cross an open meadow that sports several small tarns. Then climb steadily to a rocky saddle where you will have your first view of Ireland Lake. Enjoy a steep but easy descent southeast to open meadows on the north side of Ireland Lake. There are some campsites on the exposed meadow. Follow wilderness regulations by selecting a gravel or stony site—do not camp on fragile vegetation.

3   IRELAND LAKE TO HUTCHINGS BASIN

DISTANCE: 6.5 miles
ELEVATION GAIN/LOSS: +1880 feet / -2110 feet
TIME: 8–11 hours

If you're hiking the traverse north to south, Amelia Earhart Pass is the first pass you will encounter with scree on both sides. From the pass, a short descent leads to a basin containing several small, pretty lakes. From there, it is all rocks and slow going as you pass more lakes to Maclure Lake at the foot of the Maclure Glacier, about 3.2 miles from Ireland Lake; expect it to take three to four hours. This first rugged section of the Sierra Grand Traverse features glacier-carved tarns surrounded by steep crags and semi-permanent glaciers and snowfields.

Ahead is Russell Pass, which in some summers can be the most difficult pass on this traverse. Hidden behind the shoulder of a spur, the pass is to the right of the obvious knoll west of Maclure Glacier. The ascent to the pass includes a mixture of scree and snow bands. Conditions vary from year to year depending on snow levels; as a result, sun cups on the snow bands can range from small to huge. From the pass, you descend on loose scree and gravel-covered slopes into picturesque Hutchings Basin.

Now at the **12.9**-mile mark of your journey, begin Leg 3 by crossing open meadows southeast to the outlet creek of Ireland Lake. Cross the creek then head

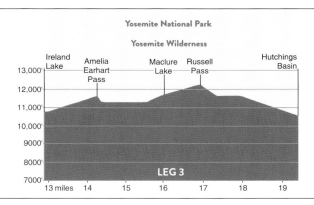

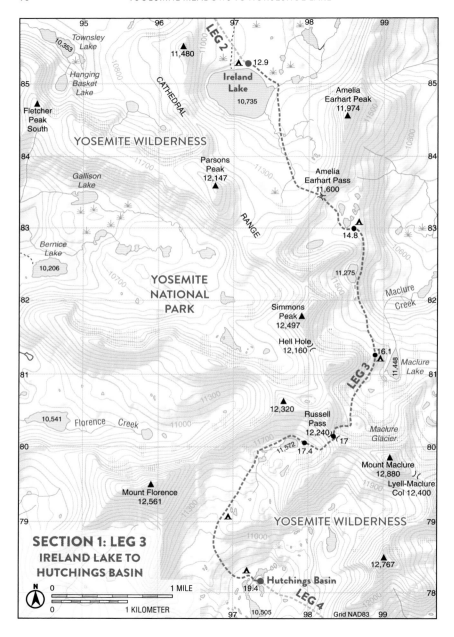

SECTION 1: LEG 3
IRELAND LAKE TO
HUTCHINGS BASIN

Tarn in Hutchings Basin

south, rising across a broad spur. Pass a small tarn in the broad gully then climb south into a rocky bowl. Above to the southeast you'll see two low points in the ridge that sweeps south from Amelia Earhart Peak. Amelia Earhart Pass is the one to the left. Climb up scree into the pass, then descend steeply on more scree to a set of tarns on a wide shelf where camping is possible.

From the southernmost tarn (**14.8**), head east then south, contouring around a steep, rocky spur to Lake 11,275. Do not be tempted to descend; instead, follow the route onto the rocky wall damming the lake. Follow the crest of the wall, pass two small tarns to the west and then climb south-southeast up a rocky ramp to a knoll overlooking Maclure Lake. About four hours from Ireland Lake with views of the Maclure Glacier, this area's campsites are limited to gravel pockets in the knoll's rocky terrain. Directly south of the knoll you can see the Maclure Glacier and above is the rocky summit of Mount Maclure. The scenery is rugged, and from below, the way ahead looks impassable for hikers.

Lake 11,275 below Simmons Peak

From the rocky knoll above Maclure Lake (**16.1**), head southwest passing to the west of a small lake. Continue southwest and then south climbing into the gully just right (west) of the obvious knoll. Depending on the amount of snow from the previous winter, your climb will vary from scree to wide bands of snow. From the gully beside the knoll, swing right (west) around the foot of a spur; directly ahead to the southwest is the pass. If the slope is covered in snow, stay on the northwestern side because there is less snow and it is less steep. Climb on scree or sun-cupped snow—time to pull out that ice axe!—to the rocks just below the ridgetop cliffs. From there, traverse very carefully left (east) across steep, loose scree for a short descent into Russell Pass. Depending on conditions, it may take you up to four hours to climb from Maclure Lake to the pass. Savor the views to the south.

From the pass (**17**), scramble 100 feet southeast up the ridge to a red rock outcrop, then descend to the right (west) into a steep chute. Watch your footing on this loose gravel and scree, which leads to the base of a red cliff below the pass. Continue descending steeply southwest then northwest on scree and slabs to the southeast end of the first lake in the basin below, Lake 11,572, which may take you about one hour from the pass. *From south to north, from Lake 11,572, climb steeply toward the red outcrop just below the pass, then scramble up the loose scree on the right to the red outcrop on the skyline.*

Walk along either shore of Lake 11,572 (**17.4**), continuing southwest; if there are remnant bands of snow, you will find the north shore easier. To avoid small bluffs, pass west of the smaller tarns. Past the tarns, the way is relatively easy on rock slabs. Descend steadily (about two hours) to the northern end of the largest lake in Hutchings Basin, Lake 10,505. On your descent, take advantage of the good views of the upper half of Sluggo Pass and plot the route ahead. You'll find good campsites near some small lakes about halfway down the descent and in the basin. In fine weather the scenery is stunning as the basin is just above tree line with many wildflowers and numerous lakes providing reflections of the surrounding peaks.

4 HUTCHINGS BASIN TO NORTH FORK SAN JOAQUIN RIVER

DISTANCE: 4.8 miles
ELEVATION GAIN/LOSS: +2440 feet / -2840 feet
TIME: 7½–9 hours

Nearly a mile southeast of Lake 10,505, Sluggo Pass—with a steep, narrow gully filled with loose scree—looks daunting. The climb is much easier than it appears because you can avoid the steepest section of the gully by climbing the rocky buttress on its left. From the pass, follow an easy descent to the lake basin at the head of the Lyell Fork Merced River. This basin is higher and rockier than Hutchings Basin. From here, you can choose the alternate route, which rejoins Leg 5 about midway (see sidebar, "Alternate Route: Blue Lake and Bench Canyon") or you can continue on the main route.

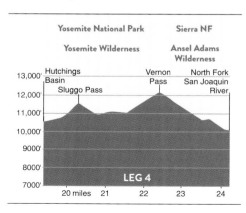

The route over Vernon Pass is spectacular, passing through a wild, rugged landscape. From the valley, Vernon Pass, about

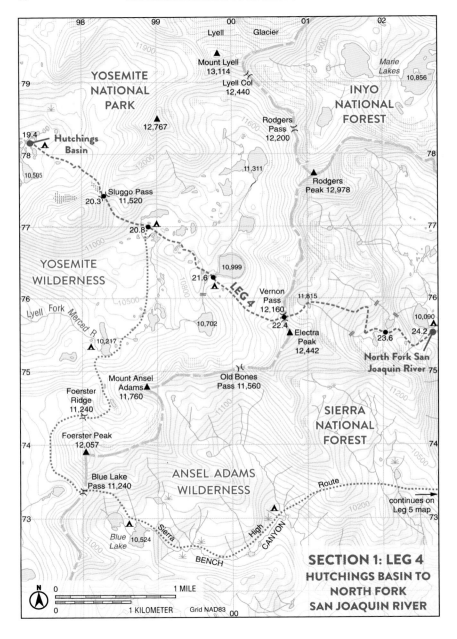

SECTION 1: LEG 4
HUTCHINGS BASIN TO
NORTH FORK
SAN JOAQUIN RIVER

Rocky gully leading to Sluggo Pass

500 feet left (north) of the summit of Electra Peak, is not obvious. From the bowl, Electra Peak is southeast (left) of a red knoll. The climb to the pass is not hard but is a long, tedious ascent on scree almost the entire way. Vernon Pass provides a great view of the Sierra range to the west with a distant but clear view of Half Dome in Yosemite Valley. The descent from the pass to the North Fork San Joaquin River is steep and requires some routefinding. The North Fork is an awesome place with rugged, colorful scenery.

From Lake 10,505 (**19.4**), head east-southeast up rock and scree into a bowl containing a tarn. Follow the grassy ramp rising from right to left (south to north) then climb onto the rocky spur just left of the narrow, scree-filled gully. The spur has a series of small, grass-covered ledges and is a straightforward but steep scramble. Follow the rocky rib, climbing as high as possible, then exit right into the now gently angled gully. From there, scree and snow bands lead to the top of Sluggo Pass, which may take you about two hours from Lake 10,505.

From Sluggo Pass (**20.3**), descend easily south-southeast on scree into a small meadow. You'll then follow more scree that leads into another meadow. Veer left (southeast) to follow a grassy lead down to the first lake in the basin below, which may be about one hour from the pass. You can camp here. At this point, you can choose to forego a trek over Vernon Pass for an alternate route (see sidebar) that joins the main traverse at the 25.3-mile mark in Leg 5.

As you continue on the main traverse (**20.8**), head southeast by scrambling over moraine ridges and passing several small tarns to the outlet of Lake 10,999.

Rock-bound lake in Hutchings Basin

Cross the outlet creek to a small tarn in a grassy bowl southeast of Lake 10,999. Terraces near the bowl provide an exposed, scenic campsite. This rarely visited lake basin is above tree line and features stark scenery of rock-bound lakes and peaks. If time allows, explore the higher lakes to the northeast at the head of the valley.

From the bowl near Lake 10,999 (**21.6**) head southeast climbing the wide, scree-covered spur toward Electra Peak, avoiding the steepest sections. Near the top, the scree steepens, so veer to the right (south) onto a spur crest and follow it east to Vernon Pass.

The easiest descent from the pass (**22.4**) is about 50 feet south of the lowest point. Descend east and follow a ramp through a short cliff line onto large scree, then swing left (northeast), descending steep scree to two small rock-bound lakes

ALTERNATE ROUTE: BLUE LAKE AND BENCH CANYON

The nearby Sierra High Route (SHR) passes scenic Blue Lake, then descends the gentle and pretty valley of Bench Canyon. This alternate route crosses two passes before joining the SHR and is 3.5 miles (and at least five hours) longer than the Sierra Grand Traverse. From the tarns at 20.8 miles to rejoining the traverse midway in Leg 5, you'll hike 7 miles and cross Foerster Ridge and Blue Lake Pass, which hug the north and south sides of Foerster Peak. In the entire route, you'll gain 2300 feet of elevation while losing 3500 feet.

From the northernmost lake in the Lyell Fork Merced River basin (**20.8**), head south, descending toward Lake 10,217. Cross the inlet creek above the lake, follow the lake's south shore, then turn left (south) and climb scree into the hanging valley above. Mount Ansel Adams is looming above to the east. Continue up scree in the valley until a ramp on the right (west) leads to a bench on the spur above rocky outcrops. You've arrived at Foerster Ridge, which—you'd never know from its name—is a pass. From the pass, continue on the same level around to the western slopes of Foerster Peak, rise to a white outcrop, then climb gently south, crossing several bands of scree to join the SHR at Blue Lake Pass. From the pass descend eastward on rocky ramps to the head of a grass-filled gully and then descend the gully to Blue Lake. Despite the singular name, there are two lakes and you can find campsites near both. You're in a great spot for sunset views of the Ritter Range to the east.

From Blue Lake take a relatively easy walk for 1.5 miles down the U-shaped Bench Canyon. When the valley swings around to the southeast, leave it by heading northeast, climbing steeply for 1100 feet to cross a spur, then continue eastward to Twin Island Lakes; you're now almost back to the traverse. Follow the east side of the southernmost lake, descend to the northern, lower lake, and halfway along its eastern shore, turn right (east) to pass through a small saddle to a bench. Follow the bench northeast to rejoin the Sierra Grand Traverse at the **25.3**-mile point.

below the pass. Sometimes the lakes are covered with ice and snow. From the lakes, head eastward down the center of a wide, stony slope for 0.4 mile to the top of a high cliff and a view of a waterfall toward the right (south). Turn left (northeast) following the cliff edge, descend gently into a narrow gully, then turn right (south) and descend the gully to the base of the cliff. Follow the creek in the valley, passing below the waterfall, to a lake, then continue to a second, larger lake. On the northeast side of this lake the outlet tumbles into another high waterfall.

Just before the lake (**23.6**), climb the short, steep slope on the eastern side of the lake to a crest, which sometimes has a steep snowbank. From the crest head southeast, descending steadily past a small tarn and into the top of a broad gully. Turn left (northeast) descending into the gully and follow it northeast to just below Lake 10,090. Headwaters of the North Fork San Joaquin River, the lake is in a rugged basin of red and gray sedimentary rock. This rock lies above the granite base of the range and fossils have been found in this valley. You can find campsites below the lake.

5 NORTH FORK SAN JOAQUIN RIVER TO THOUSAND ISLAND LAKE

DISTANCE: 4.8 miles
ELEVATION GAIN/LOSS: +2070 feet / -2340 feet
TIME: 6½–8 hours

Following the North Fork San Joaquin River downstream to a gorge is a delightful walk. Some boulders provide an unexpected yet very welcome river crossing, and soon after, you meet and then follow the Sierra High Route through to the Mine Site, which has two main areas. Find one by scrambling up the cliff west of the campsite and the other farther east around the corner of the cliff where a defined trail climbs into a cutting in the cliff. The traverse continues following the footsteps of the Sierra High Route through the rocky North Glacier Pass and then descends to the scenic Thousand Island Lake. You'll need to climb one class 3 section, a short scramble onto a ledge.

Start this leg at the **24.2**-mile mark by following the southern bank of the river downstream for 0.7 mile into the top of a gorge about 0.4 mile before

Twin Island Lakes. Just below a waterfall, cross the river on large boulders. From there, descend a gentle gully southward toward the saddle to the left (northeast) of the knoll above Twin Island Lakes. Cross a side creek, then climb gently into the saddle. A short, rocky descent follows to meet the use trail of the Sierra High Route (**25.3**); your journey from Lake

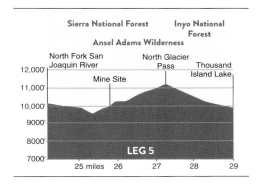

10,090 may be about two hours. If you took the alternate route, this is where you rejoin the Sierra Grand Traverse.

Lake 10,090 along the North Fork San Joaquin River

Turn left and follow the use trail, initially descending a gully, then veer left (southeast) to follow a grassy lead. Ignore a short climb on the left to an obvious saddle and continue descending to the next set of benches. The unmarked use trail then heads eastward, sidling up and down across slopes below bluffs until about 300 feet before a waterfall. The well-defined use trail then starts switch-backing up to a bench below a cliff. Follow the bench east to a group of trees that provide a semi-sheltered campsite. This is the site of a former mine with pieces of machinery and cables scattered about and some cuttings in the bluff above.

The Mine Site is near a creek junction (**25.8**). The creek flowing from Lake Catherine is on the right (southeast), but cliffs block a direct route up the valley. Instead, the route follows the left-hand creek north on a well-defined use trail, which soon braids, becoming less defined. Find your way by climbing up the

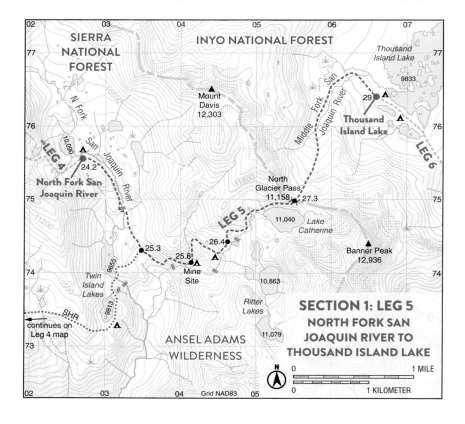

Climbing the class 3 step up to North Glacier Pass

valley to the base of a bluff of red rock to the east (right). Climb onto the red bluff or continue just past it, then back right to the top of the bluff. From the top head southeast, descend briefly to a wide meadow. You can find places to camp here, but it's exposed. From the meadow, the route stays on the north side of the creek. Climb up scree to a small lake and waterfall.

Above is a steep bluff (**26.4**), which you'll encounter about 300 feet before the waterfall. From there, you'll need to do a short, class 3 step onto a ledge. You'll then find easier, class 2 scrambling that leads onto open, sloping slabs. Head eastward back toward the creek. Switchback your way up more slabs and rocky outcrops on the northwest side of the creek to pass a small lake and soon after the outlet of Lake Catherine. Continue along the north shore of the lake then climb northeast up scree into North Glacier Pass. You'll have good views of the glacier on Banner Peak. A small bowl in the pass provides shelter in windy weather.

From North Glacier Pass (**27.3**) head northeast, descending steeply on scree. Follow a use trail to easier terrain in a valley. Continue following unmarked use trails north then northeast as you steadily descend. Leave the use trail and head southeast cross-country to the southwestern end of Thousand Island Lake. This is a popular camping area and scattered campsites are plentiful. While you will enjoy the good views at sunset, sunrise can be special with alpenglow on Banner Peak reflected in tarns, so be sure you get up early! Note that camping is prohibited at the northeastern end of Thousand Island Lake.

6   THOUSAND ISLAND LAKE TO MINARET LAKE

DISTANCE: 6 miles
ELEVATION GAIN/LOSS: +1620 feet / -1660 feet
TIME: 6–7½ hours

The traverse along the eastern foot of the Ritter Range is one of this route's most delightful sections. While you will cross several passes, there are no long climbs or descents, nor extended sections of scree, but you will have views of pretty lakes, and along the way, the spectacular spires of The Minarets tower above you. The traverse leads to the very popular Minaret Lake.

After a refreshing night at Thousand Island Lake (**29**), with Banner Peak as your backdrop, walk southeast following the low ridge between Thousand Island Lake and a series of small lakes. Cross the inlet creek of Thousand Island Lake,

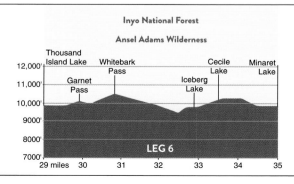

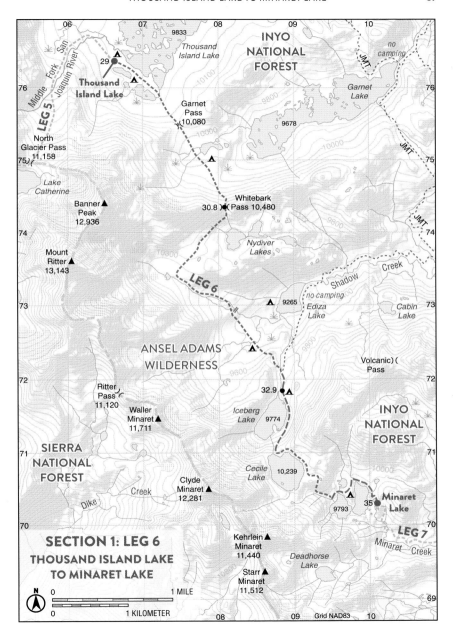

SECTION 1: LEG 6
THOUSAND ISLAND LAKE TO MINARET LAKE

then climb gradually southeast into Garnet Pass. A short descent leads to some small lakes on a meadow above Garnet Lake to the northeast. You'll find scattered campsites in the area and the sunrise reflections here are just as good as those near Thousand Island Lake. Like Thousand Island Lake, camping is banned at the northeastern end of Garnet Lake. Continue southeast, climbing a scree slope to Whitebark Pass. The slope steepens toward the top, and if there is snow keep to the east side.

From Whitebark Pass (**30.8**) descend scree until it is possible to turn right and contour southwest across the slopes above Nydiver Lakes where the angle of the slope soon relents. Cross a wide bench, passing some small tarns, and descend into a high meadow. Head southeast directly toward the outlet of Iceberg Lake.

Sunrise on Banner Peak

Nydiver Lakes from Whitebark Pass

This steady descent passes through open whitebark forest to a meadow. Continue for 0.8 mile, rounding one spur to cross a small saddle on a spur and soon meet the well-defined trail from Ediza Lake to Iceberg Lake. Continue right and follow the marked trail southward to the outlet of Iceberg Lake.

Follow the unmarked trail on the eastern shore of Iceberg Lake (**32.9**) as you climb steeply to the outlet of Cecile Lake. Follow the shoreline to the lake's east side. From here you can descend very steeply to the creek that leads to Minaret Lake; however, a much easier alternative is to continue east for about 300 feet, cross a small rise, then descend south into the valley below. From there, follow the creek southeast to arrive at the northwest shore of Minaret Lake. *If you are traveling south to north, turn around if you meet the cliff at the top of the creek, and go back 300 feet to find the easier gully to the northeast.* Follow the Minaret Lake shoreline to the lake's eastern shore. If there are no snowbanks, you can walk along the southern side.

Because of the nearly unparalleled views of the Minaret peaks, the lake is a popular backcountry destination for overnighters coming in from Reds Meadow.

Even though there will be others sharing the place, it remains a picturesque camping location, and if you hunt around you'll sometimes find a quieter nook away from crowds. There are awe-inspiring views all around and they are even better at sunrise, so be sure to wake in time to enjoy the moment.

7 MINARET LAKE TO REDS MEADOW

DISTANCE: 7.7 miles
ELEVATION GAIN/LOSS: +120 feet / -2270 feet
TIME: 3–4 hours

The end point of Leg 7 is in the deep valley of the Middle Fork San Joaquin River, which cuts north-south through the high country of the Sierra Nevada east of Mammoth Lakes. The Sierra Grand Traverse takes the shortest route from the west to cross the river valley to the continuation of the high country east of the river by following trails directly to Reds Meadow.

From the eastern shore of Minaret Lake (**35**), follow the marked trail along the northern side of Minaret Creek descending steadily for 5.3 miles to meet the John Muir Trail (JMT) in Johnston Meadow.

Turn right (southeast, **40.3**) and follow the JMT for 1.5 miles; at this junction take a left, following a good trail that descends toward Devils Postpile National Monument. Cross a bridge in the valley, turn right, and follow the signposted trail passing below the Devils Postpile. This geologic wonder, a set of basalt columns that resulted from a lava flow that cooled quickly with cracks forming

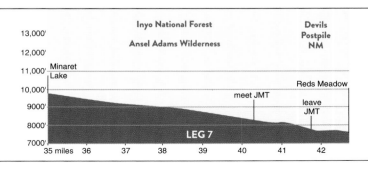

The fascinating basalt columns at Devils Postpile National Monument

when it contracted, is popular since it is one of the few sites in the US where basalt columns can be seen. If you have time, the short side trip to the top of the columns is rewarding; you can see the column cracks in the pavement created by glacial action.

Return to the main trail and continue southeast, keep left at the Rainbow Falls trail junction, and rise gently to cross the road to Reds Meadow where there is a campground with nearby hot springs and showers. Food supplies can be sent to the nearby Red's Meadow Resort (a fee applies). If planning an overnight stop in

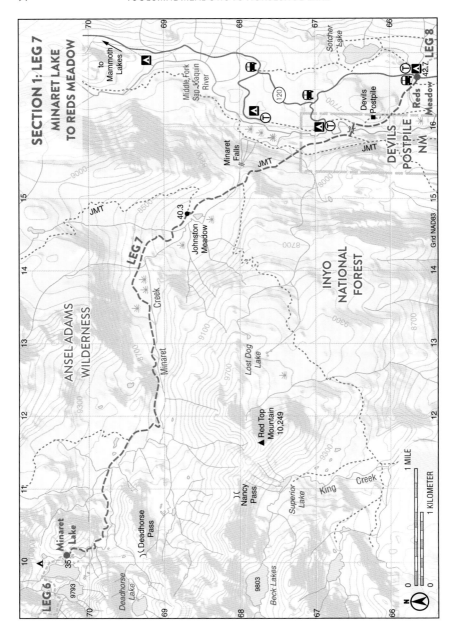

SECTION 1: LEG 7
MINARET LAKE
TO REDS MEADOW

Meadow near Devils Postpile

Mammoth Lakes, a shuttle bus operates multiple times daily from Reds Meadow to Mammoth Lakes during summer. The alternative is to continue walking over Mammoth Pass to Horseshoe Lake, where a free shuttle bus runs to Mammoth Lakes township.

8 REDS MEADOW TO HORSESHOE LAKE

DISTANCE: 4.2 miles
ELEVATION GAIN/LOSS: +1670 feet / -420 feet
TIME: 2–2½ hours

The trail from Reds Meadow to Horseshoe Lake passes through a section of forest that was damaged by fire in 1992 but is slowly recovering. You can skip this section by taking the shuttle bus from Reds Meadow to Mammoth Lakes. By using

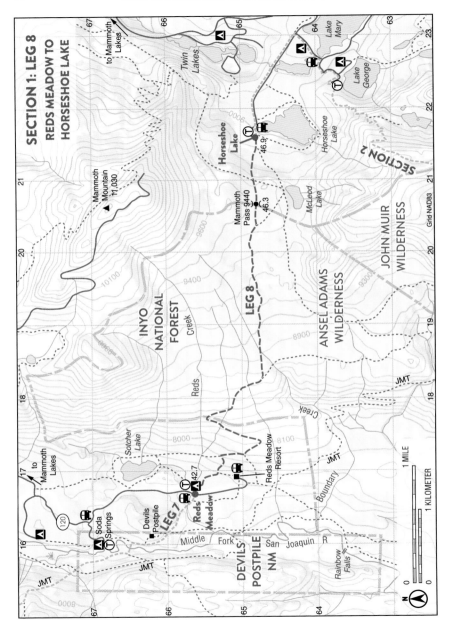

the free shuttle bus from Mammoth Lakes to Lake George Road you can then begin Section 2 of the Sierra Grand Traverse.

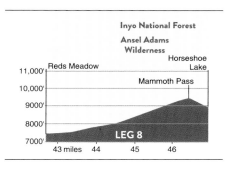

From the southeast end of the Reds Meadow campground (**42.7**) follow a trail south and almost immediately turn left (east) onto a little-used trail. Climb to meet a more defined trail from Sotcher Lake. Turn right (south) and follow it to a junction, turn left (southeast), and climb gently, following some long switchbacks to the next junction. Turn left again (east) and climb steadily through fire-damaged forest. The trail leads into dense pine forest in the region surrounding Mammoth Pass. Continue east from the pass (**46.3**) descending steadily to the parking area beside Horseshoe Lake. The town of Mammoth Lakes can be accessed from here by using the free Lakes Basin Trolley.

The Minarets from trail to Mammoth Pass

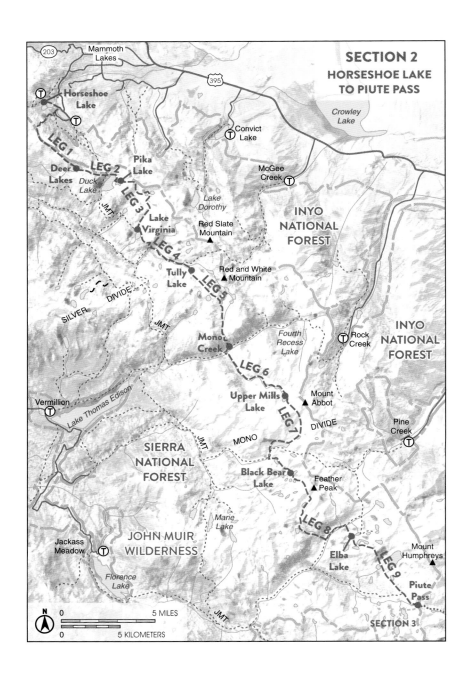

203
Mammoth
Lakes
395

Horseshoe
Lake

LEG 1

Convict
Lake

Crowley
Lake

Pika
Lake

LEG 2

Deer
Lakes

Duck
Lake

McGee
Creek

LEG 3

JMT

Lake
Dorothy

INYO
NATIONAL
FOREST

Lake
Virginia

Red Slate
▲ Mountain

LEG 4

Red and White
▲ Mountain

Tully
Lake

LEG 5

DIVIDE

SILVER

JMT

Fourth
Recess
Lake

Rock
Creek

INYO
NATIONAL
FOREST

Mono
Creek

LEG 6

Vermillion

Lake Thomas Edison

Upper Mills
Lake

LEG 7

Mount
▲ Abbot

DIVIDE

Pine
Creek

SIERRA
NATIONAL
FOREST

JMT

MONO

Black Bear
Lake

Feather
▲ Peak

Jackass
Meadow

Marie
Lake

JOHN MUIR
WILDERNESS

LEG 8

Elba
Lake

Mount
Humphreys
▲

LEG 9

Piute
Pass

Florence
Lake

N

0   5 MILES

0   5 KILOMETERS

JMT

SECTION 3

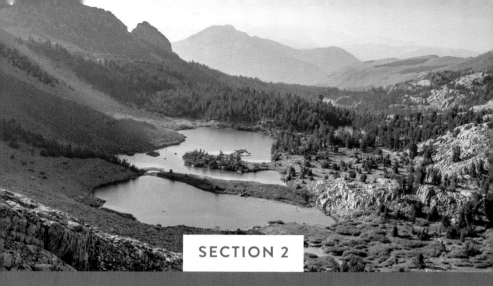

SECTION 2

HORSESHOE LAKE TO PIUTE PASS

DISTANCE: 48.8 miles
TIME: 5 to 10 days
ON-TRAIL: 19.6 miles
OFF-TRAIL: 29.2 miles
ELEVATION GAIN: +15,500 feet
ELEVATION LOSS: -12,970 feet
LOW POINT: 8580 feet
HIGH POINT: 12,360 feet
MAPS: Harrison: Mammoth High Country, Mono Divide High Country; USGS: Crystal Crag, Bloody Mountain, Graveyard Peak, Mount Abbot, Mount Hilgard, Mount Tarn, Mount Darwin

PERMITS & REGULATIONS

Obtain a new wilderness permit from the Inyo National Forest office in Mammoth

Lakes for a Deer Lakes entry if you take any zero days. The inlet creek to Lake Virginia on the JMT can be difficult to cross at high water levels.

LEGS

1. Horseshoe Lake to Deer Lakes
2. Deer Lakes to Pika Lake
3. Pika Lake to Lake Virginia
4. Lake Virginia to Tully Lake
5. Tully Lake to Mono Creek
6. Mono Creek to Upper Mills Lake
7. Upper Mills Lake to Black Bear Lake
8. Black Bear Lake to Elba Lake
9. Elba Lake to Piute Pass

ABOVE: *View from Duck Pass (Leg 2)*

This section of the Sierra Grand Traverse passes through many beautiful high lake basins; the terrain is not as rugged as the Cathedral Range in Section 1. The lake basins are open with scenic views of distant peaks. The traverse primarily follows the Sierra High Route (SHR) with some alternate routes. The first alternate is from Duck Pass past the scenic lakes of Pika, Ram, Glen, and Glennette. The second alternate route skips Izaak Walton Lake by passing through Horse Canyon, the traverse's only narrow slot gorge. A third possible alternate route for those who have walked the Sierra High Route is from Lake Italy, crossing Italy, Pine, and Steelhead Passes to Humphreys Basin, but this option misses the more scenic route through the Bear Lakes Basin.

ACCESS

This section can be accessed from Horseshoe Lake on the north end and Piute Pass on the south end.

North: Horseshoe Lake

The Lakes Basin Trolley, a free shuttle bus service that operates daily from 9 AM to 6 PM from early July until late September, runs past Horseshoe Lake and Lake George Road daily about twice every hour. Always check the website to be sure it's running when you need it as the summer season start and end dates of the service are affected by snow levels (see Resources). Use the Lakes Basin Trolley to get you to and from Mammoth Lakes for the start of this section; several other free buses also run around Mammoth Lakes, giving you easy opportunity to gather everything for your resupply.

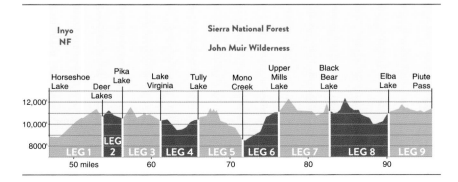

Horse Canyon (Leg 4), the only slot canyon on the traverse

Mammoth Lakes is a good resupply point. With a resident population of around eight thousand, it has good services such as restaurants, overnight accommodations, supermarkets, and several outdoor retailers. Some hotels and other accommodations will store excess baggage, including food resupply packages if you are booked to stay there. Mammoth Lakes is a ski resort in winter and in summer is a center for mountain bike riding and hiking. Expect resort prices for some services.

South: Piute Pass

From Piute Pass, follow a marked trail 5 miles eastward to the road and day visitor parking lot near North Lake; this is the closest road access point to the Sierra Grand Traverse since Mammoth Lakes. From the pass, the trail descends steadily, passing several lakes. Established campsites are at Piute Lake and Loch Leven. After passing Loch Leven, the trail heads away from the creek to the top of a switchbacking descent and then heads southeast into forest. The trail follows the valley to the road and parking lot; there's a camping area near North Lake.

When you arrive at the road, follow it eastward 0.8 mile to the hikers parking area or, if catching the Bishop Lake Shuttle at Lake Sabrina, follow the road eastward an additional 1.2 miles to the camping area and road junction to Lake Sabrina. From North Lake, it is 19.8 miles by road to Bishop, the closest town. With a population of nearly four thousand, Bishop is a reliable resupply point. You'll find restaurants, overnight accommodations, supermarkets, and several outdoor retailers.

Connecting Trails

Through this section, all of the potential exit routes are to the east and are about one day's walk from the Sierra Grand Traverse. From the start of the section at Horseshoe Lake to Lake Virginia (Legs 1 to 3), the shortest route is to return to Mammoth Lakes along the John Muir Trail then over Duck Pass. Between Tully Hole and Shout of Relief Pass (Legs 4 and 5), head to the trail to McGee Pass, which leads to McGee Creek, or return along the John Muir Trail and over Duck Pass as above.

From Bighorn Pass to Upper Mills Lake (Legs 5 to 6), follow the Mono Creek Trail over Mono Pass to Rock Creek. From Lake Italy (Leg 7), you can follow an old unmaintained trail over Italy Pass to Pine Creek. In the Bear Lakes Basin (Leg 8), Granite Bear Pass, which is due east of Black Bear Lake, provides an off-trail, direct route to Granite Park to join trails heading to Pine Creek. From Feather Pass to Carol Col (Legs 8 and 9), the French Canyon Trail leads over Pine Creek Pass and on to Pine Creek.

1   HORSESHOE LAKE TO DEER LAKES

DISTANCE: 6.8 miles
ELEVATION GAIN/LOSS: +2500 feet / -710 feet
TIME: 3½–4½ hours

The section starts with a 1.3-mile walk beside a road from Horseshoe Lake to Lake George Road, which you can avoid by using the free shuttle bus. Initially this leg

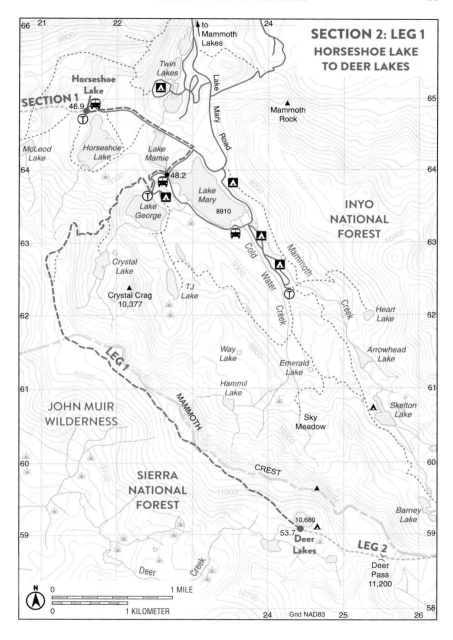

SECTION 2: LEG 1
HORSESHOE LAKE TO DEER LAKES

Reflections in Deer Lakes

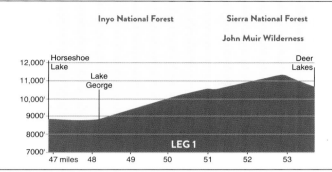

is a steep climb to Mammoth Crest, but your efforts are rewarded with sweeping views of Mammoth Lakes township and the Ritter Range.

From Horseshoe Lake (**46.9**), follow the footpath on the north side of the road eastward for 1 mile and then turn right and follow the road on the northwest side of Lake Mary for 0.3 mile to Lake George Road. This is a shuttle bus stop.

Turn right on Lake George Road (**48.2**) and follow it, keeping right at the next junction to reach the trailhead. Continue southwest along the trail toward Crystal Lake and at the first junction keep to the right (southwest), switchbacking steeply to the top of Mammoth Crest. Follow the trail south then southeast along the crest. The trail passes just south of the highest point of the crest, an unnamed point on the ridge, all of which is named Mammoth Crest. Then descend steadily to the most northern of the Deer Lakes. Because of the ease of getting here, this is a popular overnight camping spot and has numerous campsites.

2   DEER LAKES TO PIKA LAKE

DISTANCE: 2.6 miles
ELEVATION GAIN/LOSS: +610 feet / -770 feet
TIME: 2–2½ hours

A relatively easy off-trail walk leads through a wide saddle to meet maintained trails at Duck Pass, from where you can follow a side trail to Pika Lake. From Deer Lakes (**53.7**), follow an unmarked trail southeast. Pass north of the highest

Sunset at Pika Lake

of the Deer Lakes, at which point the trail soon becomes indistinct. Continue southeast up a scree-covered slope heading toward an obvious gap. Pass through the gap into a sandy bowl, then continue east, climbing a little higher to cross the wide saddle of Deer Pass.

From the pass (**54.5**), continue east, descending gently for 0.7 mile to meet a trail junction on the south side of Duck Pass. At this point, you can choose to continue to Pika Lake or take an alternate route that follows the

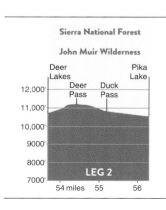

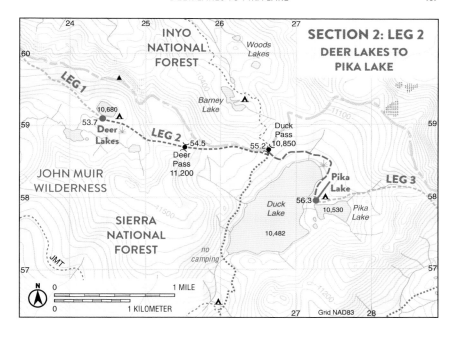

JMT and rejoins the traverse in Leg 3 (see sidebar, "Alternate Route: Duck Pass to Ram Lake via John Muir Trail").

At Duck Pass (**55.2**) continue east following a trail that descends toward Duck Lake. The trail sidles around the northern end of the lake and then along the east shore to Pika Lake. You'll find numerous campsites in the area.

ALTERNATE ROUTE: DUCK PASS TO RAM LAKE VIA JOHN MUIR TRAIL

The alternative to the steep scree descent from Pika Pass in Leg 3 is a 4.8-mile-long diversion that follows the dusty John Muir Trail (JMT). You'll gain 1000 feet in elevation but lose 1300 feet as you descend to Purple Lake and walk north at the foot of an unnamed crest to your west. Taking this route may be a three- to four-hour walk.

From Duck Pass (**55.2**), follow the marked trail southwest, sidling steep, open slopes above Duck Lake. Enjoy good views across the lake. Continue descending steadily to the outlet of Duck Lake at its southwest corner. Camping is not allowed around the outlet. Cross the outlet, then descend, following a trail that switchbacks through granite slabs and open forest to meet the JMT; camping is an option here. Head left (south) on the JMT, following it for the next 2 miles. The well-used and at times dusty trail continues south, rising to cross a wide spur, then swings eastward to descend to Purple Lake.

Just before the lake, an unmarked trail on the left leads to campsites in sheltered forest. Camping is prohibited near the lake outlet. The unmarked trail continues to the northeast and fades out before joining the Sierra Grand Traverse below and southeast of Pika Pass. Rejoin the traverse to head east up the valley to Ram Lake.

3   PIKA LAKE TO LAKE VIRGINIA

DISTANCE: 4.8 miles
ELEVATION GAIN/LOSS: +1540 feet / -1730 feet
TIME: 5½–8 hours

A steady climb from Pika Lake leads to the scree-filled Pika Pass. The descent is quite steep, so some groups might prefer to follow the longer but easier alternative route via the John Muir Trail to Purple Lake (see sidebar, "Alternate Route: Duck Pass to Ram Lake via John Muir Trail"). The scenic basins containing numerous lakes, including Ram and Glen Lakes, invite exploration. Walking through the basins is easy, and you can follow any route. Leave the basin via an unnamed low-elevation pass to meet the John Muir Trail (JMT) near Lake Virginia.

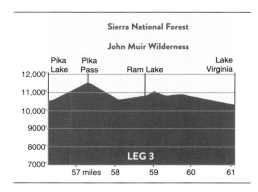

From Pika Lake (**56.3**), head east-northeast along the north shore of the lake through sparse whitebark forest, then rise onto scree-covered slopes. Follow the

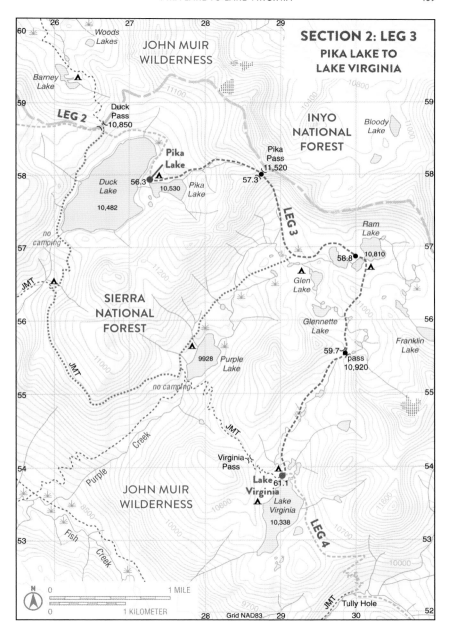

SECTION 2: LEG 3
PIKA LAKE TO
LAKE VIRGINIA

60

JOHN MUIR
WILDERNESS

Woods
Lakes

Barney
Lake

59

LEG 2

Duck
Pass
10,850

INYO
NATIONAL
FOREST

Bloody
Lake

Pika
Lake

Pika
Pass
11,520

58

Duck
Lake
10,482

56.3

10,530

Pika
Lake

57.3

LEG 3

Ram
Lake

no
camping

57

58.8

10,810

JMT

Glen
Lake

SIERRA
NATIONAL
FOREST

56

Glennette
Lake

Franklin
Lake

JMT

9928

Purple
Lake

59.7

pass
10,920

55

no camping

Creek

JMT

54

Purple

Virginia
Pass

JOHN MUIR
WILDERNESS

Lake
Virginia

61.1

Lake
Virginia
10,338

LEG 4

53

Fish

Creek

N

0   1 MILE

0   1 KILOMETER

JMT

Tully Hole

52

Grid NAD83

Tarn near Glennette Lake

broad gully and near the top swing southeast into Pika Pass. The ascent climbs a lot of scree but is not difficult.

The descent on the east side of Pika Pass (**57.3**) is a little more challenging. Descend steeply southeast into some narrow chutes, then continue descending very steeply on loose scree. At lower elevation the descent eases. From this broadly open area, begin to head eastward along the valley, rounding one large lake on its north side to arrive at Ram Lake. Campsites are available in the valley. Take any route from Ram Lake (**58.8**) to Glennette Lake, but the direct route straight south climbs over a low spur. From Glennette Lake continue south, rising gently to an unnamed pass at 10,920 feet.

From the pass (**59.7**), descend steadily southwest following a creek and passing several tarns before meeting the JMT just before you arrive at Lake Virginia. The grass near the lake is a popular campsite with JMT hikers. You'll find sheltered campsites away from the lake in nearby forest.

4   LAKE VIRGINIA TO TULLY LAKE

DISTANCE: 4.9 miles
ELEVATION GAIN/LOSS: +1180 feet / -930 feet
TIME: 3–4 hours

The Sierra Grand Traverse follows the John Muir Trail (JMT) for the next 1.4 miles to Tully Hole. The traverse leaves the JMT and follows a marked trail past a meadow before climbing through the narrow Horse Canyon to Tully Lake leaving defined trails. Most of this leg passes through a mixture of forests and meadows. Horse Canyon is the only slot canyon on the traverse.

Tully Lake

Horse Heaven

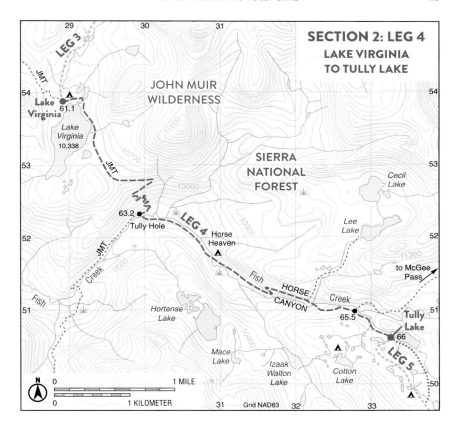

From Lake Virginia (**61.1**), follow the JMT eastward, crossing the lake's inlet streams. At high water levels these crossings can be difficult. Follow the eastern shoreline south around the lake then head southeast, rising through open forest into a broad saddle. Cross the saddle to open slopes where there is a good view of Tully Hole. Follow the benched JMT zigzagging down the open, stony slope into the valley, and cross the stream to a trail junction in Tully Hole. Tully Hole has a large meadow but few camp here as mosquitos are common. It is named after a forest ranger, Gene Tully, who, between 1905 and 1907, played a large role in removing sheep from the Sierra. He regularly stopped to rest his horses at what is now known as Tully Hole.

At Tully Hole (**63.2**) the JMT heads southwest, while you'll head southeast toward McGee Pass; follow the well-defined trail into the flat valley of Horse Heaven. At the end of the meadow, cross a creek on a log, then start climbing. Continue to follow the trail to McGee Pass through Horse Canyon. Some zigzags lead

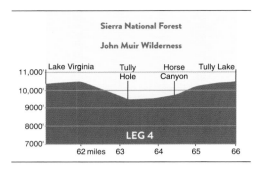

through the narrow, slot canyon. Continue to a junction with an unmarked trail on the left to Lee Lake; it's easy to miss. Rock hop across Fish Creek and continue toward McGee Pass for 0.3 mile to a signposted side trail to Tully Lake. Follow the less-used trail (**65.5**) to the right (southeast) and beside the creek to the south shore of Tully Lake.

5 | TULLY LAKE TO MONO CREEK

DISTANCE: 5.5 miles
ELEVATION GAIN/LOSS: +1280 feet / -3030 feet
TIME: 5½–6½ hours

This leg crosses two passes and has some lovely scenery. Two short alternatives are possible on this leg: The first is a more direct but less scenic climb to Shout of Relief Pass, and the second is a diversion to the scenic Grinnell Lake, a favorite of some photographers. From Laurel Lake a defined trail, mostly along Laurel Creek, descends into the forested gorge of Mono Creek to meet a trail that heads east over Mono Pass to Rock Creek.

About 300 feet past the western end of Tully Lake (**66**), turn right and climb steeply up open slopes into a short, narrow gully and climb onto the shelf above to enter a maze of small pretty lakes. Cotton Lake is farther west. You can find small campsites on rock slabs scattered throughout the area. Enjoy views of the colorful Red Slate and Red and White Mountains from this picturesque location. Continue southeast following the shelf to the last lake in the system.

Red Slate Mountain from above Tully Lake

For a short alternate route that heads directly to Shout of Relief Pass, start from the west end of Tully Lake and continue along the southwest shore of the lake, then climb the broad open valley south to meet the main route at the 67-mile mark, the last lake before the pass. Continue along the main traverse.

Two passes are in close proximity to the southernmost lake on the shelf (**67**). If you head south, you can cross Rohn Pass. The traverse crosses the other, to the southeast: Shout of Relief Pass. Climb gentle, open slopes to the pass, so named because when you hike south to north you're likely to give a shout of relief after having completed the tedious terrain from Bighorn Pass.

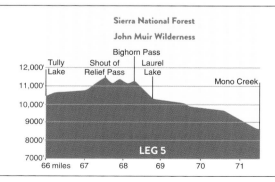

Sierra National Forest

John Muir Wilderness

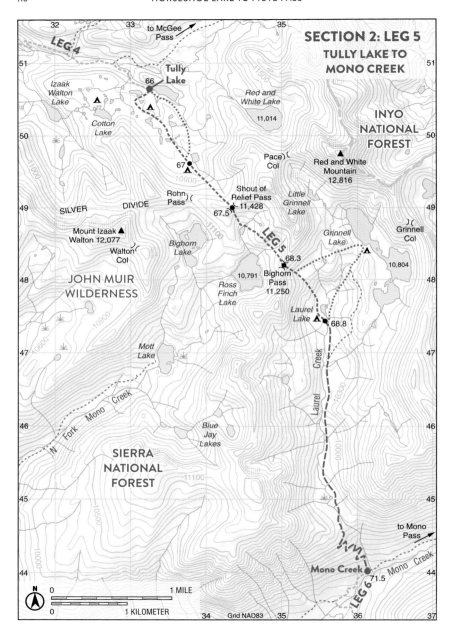

Vista from Shout of Relief Pass

From Shout of Relief Pass (**67.5**), Bighorn Pass is the next objective. This gap in the high ridge to the southeast is fairly obvious, but the route to it is not simple because a large rocky spur lies in between. There are a variety of routes between the passes with no single best route. Descend the gully from Shout of Relief for 250 vertical feet to a gully junction just above a small lake. Climb east onto the rocky spur, then descend into the wide, scree-filled gully beyond. Climb southeast to Bighorn Pass. It may take you two hours or longer to get from one pass to the other. Early explorers saw bighorn sheep in the pass, giving it the name. Savor the views from rocky outcrops just south of Bighorn Pass.

From Bighorn Pass (**68.3**), descend steeply southeast to Laurel Lake; you could take a side trip to the picturesque Grinnell Lake instead (see sidebar, "Side Trip: Grinnell Lake"). The descent from the pass is fairly easy, following open, grassy leads and the use trail ends at two obvious large boulders (glacial erratics) beside Laurel Lake. Look for good campsites near the lake, although some areas can be marshy. Follow the western shore of the lake to the outlet.

A defined trail starts near the outlet of Laurel Lake (**68.8**). Follow this south across boggy meadows to meet the junction with the trail to Grinnell Lake (see

SIDE TRIP: GRINNELL LAKE

While Laurel Lake is picturesque and may satisfy your photo needs, Grinnell Lake is considered one of the most photogenic lakes in the Sierra. You can easily visit as a side trip from the main traverse, heading to the lake from one of two ways. The walk is 1.2 miles round-trip, and you'll gain and lose 470 feet elevation.

If you've already arrived at Laurel Lake, climb the slopes to the northeast into a saddle. If you're descending from Bighorn Pass, at about one-third of the way down head northeast on a bench, then pass to the north of a tarn and contour along slopes to cross a knoll; then descend to Grinnell Lake. To continue to Laurel Lake, from the saddle on the western side of Grinnell Lake follow the access trail southwest and when it swings south, leave the trail and continue descending southwest to Laurel Lake.

sidebar). Continue south following the open valley of Laurel Creek. Very pleasant walking for 1.5 miles leads to the end of the hanging valley. The well-defined trail then descends steeply, switchbacking into the valley of Mono Creek to a trail junction. The valley of Mono Creek is a deep, narrow V-shaped valley that is characteristic of water erosion. The creeks in the side valleys are very different, having almost level valley floors and very steep sides that are the result of glaciation; then they all drop steeply into Mono Creek. This type of formation is called a hanging valley, and the side creeks of Laurel and Hopkins Creeks along with the four recesses are excellent examples.

6 | MONO CREEK TO UPPER MILLS LAKE

DISTANCE: 4.8 miles
ELEVATION GAIN/LOSS: +2590 feet / -220 feet
TIME: 4–5 hours

After a short walk along the Mono Creek Trail, the Sierra Grand Traverse climbs into the hanging valley of Second Recess and follows Mills Creek along the almost-level forested floor of this side valley. The easy walking ends abruptly with a steep climb up the valley wall following an unmarked, rough use trail

Ridge above Upper Mills Lake

into the pretty basin containing Lower and Upper Mills Lakes.

From the junction with the Mono Creek Trail (**71.5**), turn right (southeast) and follow the trail for 0.4 mile; then leave the trail by turning left (southeast) to cross the creek via a log and follow a side trail into the Second Recess. The trail climbs briefly then passes through tall

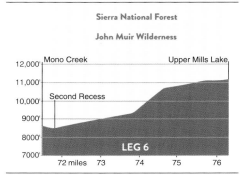

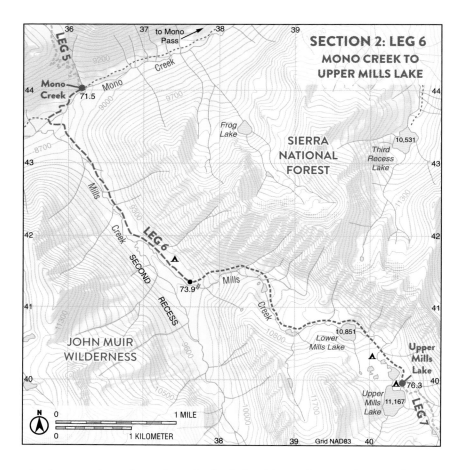

pine forest and meadows along the fairly level Second Recess for 1.4 miles to a small waterfall on Mills Creek.

At the waterfall (**73.9**) the trail leaves the Second Recess valley and starts climbing steeply eastward toward huge granite slabs. Approach the left-hand slab then swing right, crossing its foot before following a steep route up a narrow band of vegetation between two steep slabs. When the climbing eases, the very rough trail follows the northern bank of Mills Creek through sparse, scrubby forest. The valley opens up as you approach Lower Mills Lake, and easy walking up the valley leads to Upper Mills Lake. You'll find good camping spots near both lakes.

7 UPPER MILLS LAKE TO BLACK BEAR LAKE

DISTANCE: 6.4 miles
ELEVATION GAIN/LOSS: +2240 feet / -2150 feet
TIME: 7–9 hours

Gabbot Pass provides a straightforward, rocky route across Mono Divide and leads into the barren high lake basin of Lake Italy. Lake Italy is large and not as scenic as many High Sierra lakes, but the stream and small cascades below the lake are beautiful and make up for the less interesting walk along the lakeshore. The last part of this leg is a steep climb to White Bear Pass. While the pass looks intimidating, there are no bluffs or hidden obstacles; it is just a long climb up fairly stable scree to the top. An easy descent then leads to Black Bear Lake.

Morning at Black Bear Lake

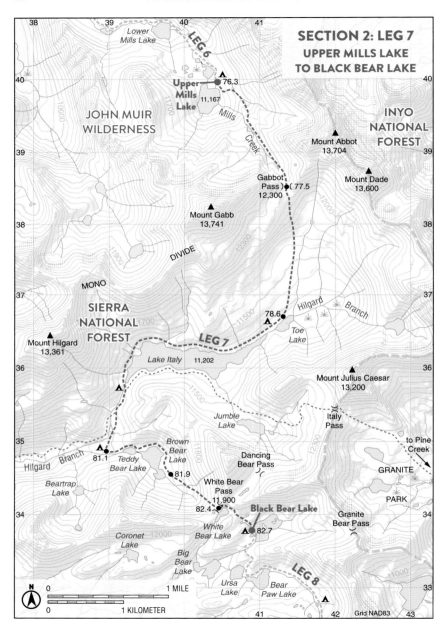

SECTION 2: LEG 7
UPPER MILLS LAKE
TO BLACK BEAR LAKE

Small lake near Gabbot Pass

From Upper Mills Lake (**76.3**) the next objective is Gabbot Pass, southeast of Upper Mills Lake and just west of Mount Abbot. Don't climb directly from Upper Mills Lake to the pass. Instead, head northeast for 500 feet then turn right (south) into a hidden, rock-filled side valley. Initially navigating the large boulders is tedious, but after a short bit, the side valley emerges onto a bench from where you'll have good views of Upper Mills Lake. From the bench follow the scree-filled gully, passing on the east side of a smaller lake, to Gabbot Pass.

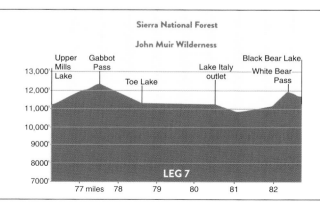

White Bear Pass from Brown Bear Lake

To descend from Gabbot Pass (**77.5**), head south on open, rock-covered slopes directly toward Toe Lake; from Upper Mills Lake, your journey may be about three hours. On the west side of Toe Lake, look for exposed camping spots.

From Toe Lake (**78.6**), follow the north and west shores of Lake Italy. You'll have mostly easy walking across grass and short stretches of scree to the outlet of the lake. Do not follow the south shore because there is a difficult section of large boulders to traverse. Cross the outlet creek of Lake Italy, then follow the stream southward, crossing numerous rock slabs. An old trail lies in this valley, and with care, you can follow it, but you don't need to since the valley is easy to walk. Continue for 0.6 mile to meet the creek that drains Teddy Bear Lake.

At this creek (**81.1**), head east, rising gently up slabs on the north side of the creek then along the north shore of Teddy Bear Lake. Continue east to pass on the north then east shores of Brown Bear Lake. You could camp in many places between Lake Italy and Brown Bear Lake.

From Brown Bear Lake (**81.9**), head up steep slopes to the southeast that lead to White Bear Pass. As you climb the scree, keep to your left, heading toward patches of vegetation. Continue climbing steeply following the vegetated bands until the slope eases, at which point you can take a direct route to the pass. The view ahead is surprising since White Bear Lake is almost at the elevation of the pass. *If you are traveling south to north, from the pass veer to your right to follow the vegetated bands; do not head straight down because that leads onto steep, glacier-polished slabs.*

Turn left (north) out of the pass (**82.4**) and follow the slopes above White Bear Lake to a saddle east of the lake. From here descend southeast passing through rocky terrain. The best route passes between two tarns to the outlet of Black Bear Lake. *If you are traveling south to north, the route from Black Bear Lake to the* *saddle is more complex since it passes through some rocky slots; near the top you might need to do some searching to find the easiest route.* You'll find established campsites near the two tarns on the descent and near Black Bear Lake.

8 BLACK BEAR LAKE TO ELBA LAKE

DISTANCE: 7.5 miles
ELEVATION GAIN/LOSS: +2290 feet / -2590 feet
TIME: 7–8½ hours

Careful navigation is required on the descent to Ursa Lake to avoid a cliff, but from there meadows lead to the inevitable scree leading to Feather Pass. From the pass descend more scree into a valley where you'll encounter several lakes and tarns before arriving at the tree line at Merriam Lake. The descent continues through scrubby forest to a large meadow, then passes through taller forest into the deep valley of French Canyon. After a short walk along French Canyon Trail, you abruptly head off-trail to climb through untracked forest to a spacious meadow near Elba Lake.

From Black Bear Lake (**82.7**), descend the broad gully of the outlet stream southwest for 100 feet, turn left (southeast), and follow a sandy bench for about 200 feet to the top of a gully. Turn right (south) and descend the grassy gully to Ursa Lake. *If you are traveling south to north, climb the gully that starts about*

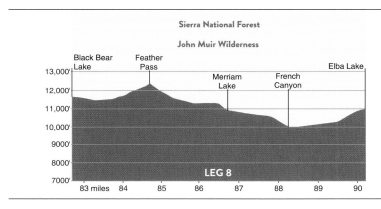

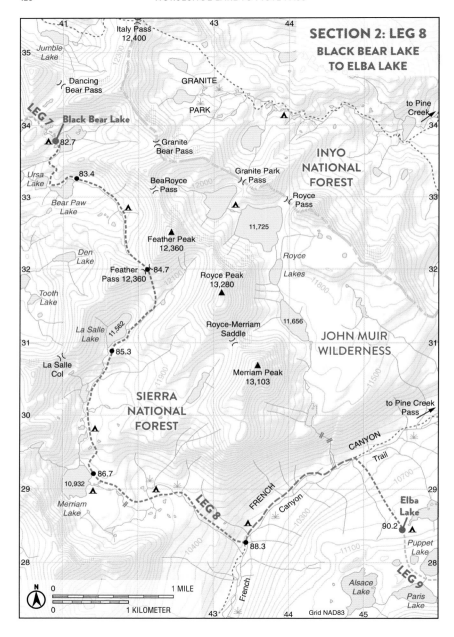

SECTION 2: LEG 8
BLACK BEAR LAKE
TO ELBA LAKE

Stunning cliffs around Ursa Lake

150 feet before the cliffs on Ursa Lake. You can find exposed campsites from Ursa Lake to the last tarn before Feather Pass.

From Ursa Lake, stay on the north side of the valley, first passing Bear Paw Lake (**83.4**) then following the wide valley southeast, south, then southeast again up rocky terrain to Feather Pass.

From Feather Pass (**84.7**), do not head south directly toward La Salle Lake. Instead, descend southeast toward the tarn above La Salle Lake along easy, rocky slopes into the shallow valley below the tarn. Turn right (southwest) and follow the outlet creek as it passes through the cliffs to La Salle Lake. Gullies to the west are steeper.

Pass La Salle Lake (**85.3**) on its eastern side by doing some small climbs and descents following ledges above the lake, then continue to follow the open valley southwest then south past a chain of small tarns. At the last tarn in the creek before Merriam Lake, veer left (slightly southeast) and rise briefly to a small tarn on a spur. Pass the tarn then turn right (southwest) and descend easily, following grassy slopes below a bluff to Merriam Lake; it may take about five and a half hours from Black Bear Lake. You can also follow the creek all the way to Merriam Lake, but it is a steeper and less scenic route.

Pass east of Merriam Lake (**86.7**) and head southeast through mixed terrain of open forest and rocks with a final descent past a cascade to a broad grassy meadow. Follow an unmarked trail northeast, then east across the meadow. This soon enters forest and descends steeply southeast to meet the well-defined French Canyon Trail.

At the trail junction (**88.3**), follow the French Canyon Trail northeast for 1.2 miles. Just past the obvious cascade that descends from Royce Lakes, leave the trail, cross the creek, and climb steeply southeast through lodgepole forest and patches of willows to an open meadow southwest of Elba Lake. Scenic campsites abound.

9 | ELBA LAKE TO PIUTE PASS

DISTANCE: 5.5 miles
ELEVATION GAIN/LOSS: +1320 feet / -840 feet
TIME: 4–5 hours

From Elba Lake an easy climb up open slopes leads to Puppet Lake on a broad bench containing several other lakes. The terrace is rocky so finding good campsites can be hard. From the bench a steep climb up scree leads into Carol Col, sometimes referred to as Puppet Pass. From there, an easy, off-trail route across the very large and open Humphreys Basin leads to the end of Section 2 at Piute Pass.

Pilot Knob and Paris Lake

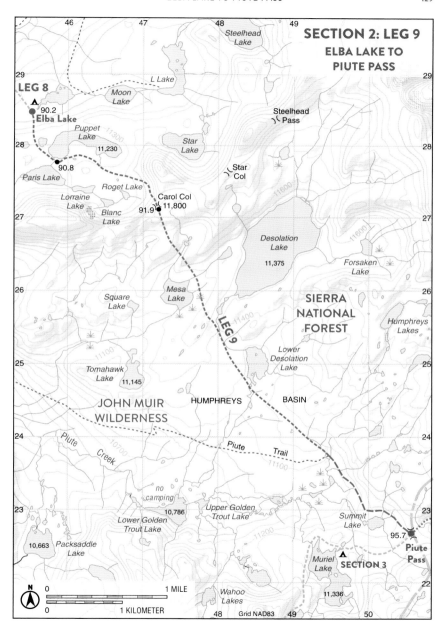

SECTION 2: LEG 9
ELBA LAKE TO
PIUTE PASS

46 47 48 49

Steelhead
Lake

L Lake

LEG 8

Moon
Lake

Steelhead
Pass

90.2
Elba Lake

Puppet
Lake

11,230

Star
Lake

Star
Col

90.8

Paris Lake

Roget Lake

Carol Col
11,800

Lorraine
Lake

Blanc
Lake

91.9

Desolation
Lake

11,375

Forsaken
Lake

Square
Lake

Mesa
Lake

SIERRA
NATIONAL
FOREST

Humphreys
Lakes

LEG 9

Lower
Desolation
Lake

Tomahawk
Lake 11,145

JOHN MUIR
WILDERNESS

HUMPHREYS

BASIN

Piute

Creek

Piute   Trail

no
camping

10,786

Lower Golden
Trout Lake

Upper Golden
Trout Lake

Summit
Lake

95.7

Piute
Pass

10,663 Packsaddle
Lake

Muriel
Lake

SECTION 3

N

0   1 MILE

0   1 KILOMETER

Wahoo
Lakes

11,336

48   Grid NAD83   49   50

Starting at Elba Lake (**90.2**), climb southward up increasingly rocky slopes to small tarns on the rocky bench east of Puppet Lake. Continue to the creek that joins Paris and Puppet Lakes. Cross the creek between the lakes (**90.8**) and head toward the north side of Roget Lake. Carol Col is above and southeast from the lake; the slopes leading to it contain a lot of large scree. The easiest route keeps to the left and climbs steeply, following the base of a small cliff. When the cliff ends, veer right and climb larger scree until you tackle a short scramble up solid rock, which leads to the pass. *Traveling south to north, start from the northern end of Carol Col and descend toward the low cliff on the right. This route avoids most of the large boulders that cover the slope directly below the pass.*

Formidable Mount Humphreys from Humphreys Basin

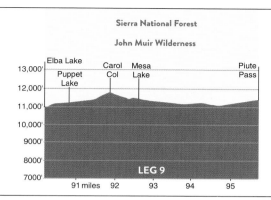

From Carol Col (**91.9**) to Piute Pass, cross the open, alpine plateau that has gently rolling ridges and scattered lakes. You can wander anywhere across the plateau—there is no preferred route. You can find many exposed camp spots in the basin. Just past Carol Col, the Sierra Grand Traverse leaves the SHR, which heads directly toward Upper Golden Trout Lake. To complete Section 2, head southeast, and when you meet the Piute Trail, continue southeast (left) following the trail to Piute Pass.

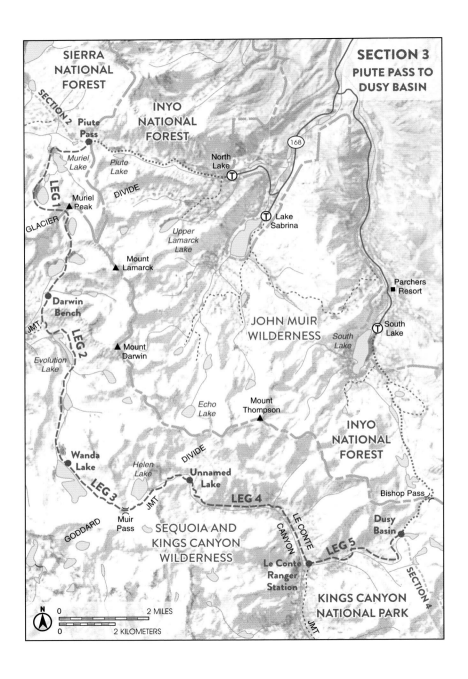

SIERRA
NATIONAL
FOREST

INYO
NATIONAL
FOREST

SECTION 2

Piute
Pass

Muriel
Lake

Piute
Lake

North
Lake

(168)

DIVIDE

Muriel
Peak

Upper
Lamarck
Lake

Lake
Sabrina

GLACIER

LEG 1

Mount
Lamarck

Parchers
Resort

JOHN MUIR
WILDERNESS

Darwin
Bench

JMT

LEG 2

South
Lake

South
Lake

Evolution
Lake

Mount
Darwin

Echo
Lake

Mount
Thompson

INYO
NATIONAL
FOREST

Wanda
Lake

DIVIDE

Helen
Lake

Unnamed
Lake

LEG 4

Bishop Pass

LEG 3

JMT

LE CONTE CANYON

Dusy
Basin

Muir
Pass

GODDARD

SEQUOIA AND
KINGS CANYON
WILDERNESS

LEG 5

SECTION 4

Le Conte
Ranger
Station

KINGS CANYON
NATIONAL PARK

JMT

N

0   2 MILES

0   2 KILOMETERS

PIUTE PASS TO DUSY BASIN

DISTANCE: 24.5 miles
TIME: 3 to 4 days
ON-TRAIL: 18.3 miles
OFF-TRAIL: 6.2 miles
ELEVATION GAIN: +5070 feet
ELEVATION LOSS: -5120 feet
LOW POINT: 8700 feet
HIGH POINT: 12,350 feet
MAPS:: Harrison: Mono Divide High Country, Kings Canyon High Country; USGS: Mount Darwin, Mount Goddard, North Palisade, Mount Thompson

PERMITS & REGULATIONS

Obtain a new wilderness permit from the Inyo National Forest office in Bishop for a North Lake entry if you take any zero days.

LEGS

1. Piute Pass to Darwin Bench
2. Darwin Bench to Wanda Lake
3. Wanda Lake to Unnamed Lake
4. Unnamed Lake to Le Conte Ranger Station
5. Le Conte Ranger Station to Dusy Basin

ABOVE: *Mount Spencer from Evolution Lake (Leg 2)*

The Sierra Grand Traverse rises into the scree-filled basin of Goethe Lake. A tedious scree-hop over Alpine Col leads to the beautiful alpine shelf known as Darwin Bench. The traverse then continues by following the John Muir Trail (JMT) over Muir Pass into Le Conte Canyon. Traveling over Muir Pass provides the most direct walking route to cross

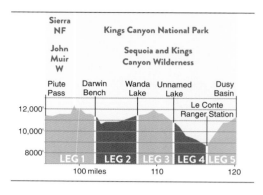

the Goddard Divide; the alternatives are convoluted, winding routes requiring long descents and ascents.

Evolution Lake and Muir Pass are must-see destinations even though you will meet many other backpackers on this section of the JMT. While similar to many other high lake basins and passes along the traverse, this area is one of the most scenic. The section ends by leaving the John Muir Trail and climbing into the picturesque Dusy Basin.

Most groups will need to resupply before starting Section 4 to Kearsarge Pass. Take the trail northeast from Dusy Basin over Bishop Pass to South Lake. You can skip the climb to Dusy Basin by continuing to follow the JMT to Deer Meadow. However, this is a less interesting walk since the JMT stays in forest in the valley.

ACCESS

This section can be accessed from Piute Pass on the north end and Dusy Basin on the south end.

North: Piute Pass

Access Piute Pass from the east via an easy-to-follow trail from the road at North Lake; the ascent, 5 miles, could take up to four hours. To return from the end of the road at North Lake, follow the marked trail west to a trail junction. Left leads to Lamarck Lake; keep to the right. The well-defined trail passes through forest on the north side of the North Fork Bishop Creek. The trail climbs away from the creek via a series of switchbacks and then heads southwest to Loch Leven. You'll find established campsites here. Continue westward on the trail, passing several small lakes to arrive at Piute Lake where you'll find more established campsites. A final climb up open slopes leads to Piute Pass.

From North Lake, if you need to resupply or just take a zero day of rest, walk 2.2 miles to the parking lot at Lake Sabrina to grab the twice daily Bishop Creek Shuttle (which runs in summer) to Bishop, the closest town. If you walk, North Lake is 19.8 miles by road from Bishop. Bishop is a good resupply point and place to refresh; the town of four thousand has restaurants, overnight accommodations, some supermarkets, and several outdoor retailers.

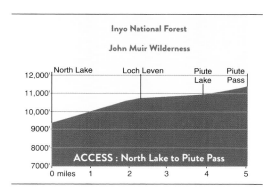

South: Dusy Basin

From Dusy Basin, walk to the closest road, which is at South Lake; the 6.9-mile walk is a descent of 2890 feet. From Dusy Basin, the

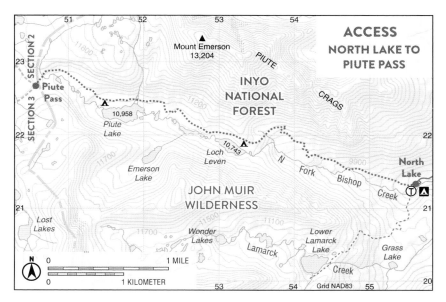

Bishop Lake from Bishop Pass via a connecting trail to South Lake

trail climbs gently northeastward for 1.2 miles to cross Bishop Pass. The well-constructed trail then switchbacks down a steep scree slope to Bishop Lake where you'll find scattered, established campsites. The trail continues northward past Saddlerock Lake, Timberline Tarns, Spearhead Lake, and Long Lake and then descends above South Lake to the parking lot at the end of the road. The twice daily Bishop Creek Shuttle operates from mid-June until late August from the parking lot to Bishop. Having your food resupply stored at Parchers Resort (a storage fee applies) is an alternative; Parchers Resort is 1.2 miles along a trail from the South Lake parking lot.

Connecting Trails

Few intermediate retreat routes are possible from this section of the traverse. From anywhere between Piute Pass and Alpine Col (Leg 1), return to Piute Pass and take the trail to North Lake (see access route, above). From Darwin Bench to Muir Pass (Legs 2 and 3), the shortest exit route enters Darwin Canyon; cross Lamarck Col then follow minor trails northeast to North Lake. From Muir Pass on (Legs 3 to 5) follow the Sierra Grand Traverse route to Dusy Basin then follow the access trail over Bishop Pass to South Lake.

1   PIUTE PASS TO DARWIN BENCH

DISTANCE: 6.3 miles
ELEVATION GAIN/LOSS: +1030 feet / -1210 feet
TIME: 6–9 hours

A leisurely half-hour walk on a marked trail leads to Muriel Lake, the closest area with established campsites near Piute Pass. From Muriel Lake almost all of the remainder of this leg is on scree. While it is fairly stable, a lot of it is medium in size, making it difficult to set a pace or rhythm. Getting to Alpine Col itself is not difficult; the most tedious sections are along lakeshores. While there are some possible campsites among rocks near Lake 11,910, continue to Darwin Bench or farther to Evolution Lake because campsites there are plentiful and more scenic.

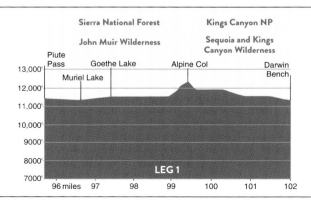

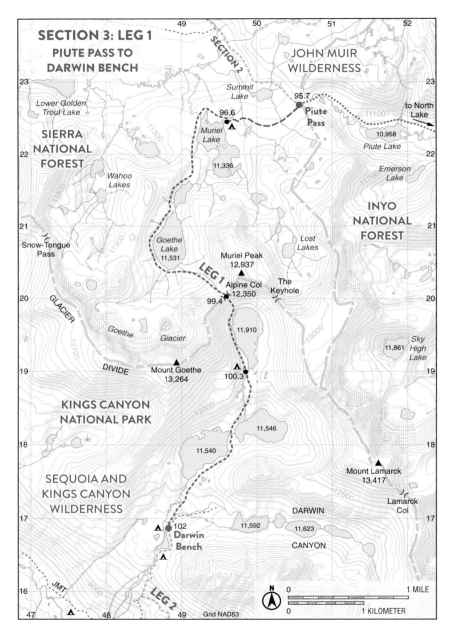

SECTION 3: LEG 1
PIUTE PASS TO
DARWIN BENCH

JOHN MUIR
WILDERNESS

Lower Golden
Trout Lake

Summit
Lake

95.7
Piute
Pass

to North
Lake

96.6

11100

Muriel
Lake

10,958

SIERRA
NATIONAL
FOREST

11,336

Piute Lake

Emerson
Lake

Wahoo
Lakes

INYO
NATIONAL
FOREST

Snow-Tongue
Pass

Goethe
Lake
11,531

Lost
Lakes

LEG 1

Muriel Peak
12,937

Alpine Col
12,350

The
Keyhole

Sky
High
Lake

99.4

11,861

GLACIER

Goethe

Glacier

11,910

13000

20

DIVIDE

Mount Goethe
13,264

100.3

KINGS CANYON
NATIONAL PARK

11,546

11,540

Mount Lamarck
13,417

SEQUOIA AND
KINGS CANYON
WILDERNESS

102
Darwin
Bench

11,592

DARWIN

11,623

Lamarck
Col

CANYON

JMT

LEG 2

Grid NAD83

N   0   1 MILE

0   1 KILOMETER

Inviting Darwin Bench

From Piute Pass (**95.7**), head west briefly to reach a trail junction. Follow the southwest trail to Muriel Lake where the marked trail ends. You'll find good campsites near the lake.

Follow the open northern and then western shores of Muriel Lake (**96.6**), continuing to head south to start climbing toward Goethe Lake. Goethe Lake is rock-bound and while the route is not difficult, progress along the western then southern shores is tedious through scree. At the south end of the lake cross the gravel flat beside the inlet creek, then start climbing eastward toward Alpine Col. You'll encounter more scree, and about halfway up, look for a band of small cliffs. Scramble up a gully in the center or on the right and continue directly to the top of the pass.

From Alpine Col (**99.4**), descend steeply southeast on scree to the rock-bound Lake 11,910. Follow the west shore by rock-hopping over extensive scree; this is not difficult, just slow. *If following the traverse south to north, follow the shoreline northward, passing underneath a rocky bluff that descends almost to the shore and then climb scree directly to the pass.* Above the southern end of the lake some scattered, single tent sites are hidden among the rocks. While you can camp here, much nicer campsites are available at Darwin Bench. Congratulations! If you've been strictly following the Sierra Grand Traverse, you've reached the halfway point. Enjoy a special treat you've been saving for just such an occasion, savor the sparkle of sun on the High Sierra lake, then keep moving!

Cross the outlet creek (**100.3**) and continue descending southward to the next two large, unnamed rock-bound lakes. Head south between Lakes 11,546 and 11,540, then continue southwest, scrambling along the eastern shore of Lake 11,540 to a smaller lake on Darwin Bench. This is a pretty area with grassy benches and scattered, scenic campsites.

2   DARWIN BENCH TO WANDA LAKE

DISTANCE: 5.4 miles
ELEVATION GAIN/LOSS: +780 feet / -600 feet
TIME: 3–4½ hours

Through sparse forest, descend following a use trail beside the creek to meet the John Muir Trail (JMT). Evolution Lake is one of the most scenic lakes on the JMT. The only detraction is that it is a popular camping area for JMT walkers, so if you hope to stay here expect to share it with a crowd. For the next 13 miles, the Sierra Grand Traverse follows the JMT. From Evolution Lake, the traverse follows a wide, glacier-carved valley passing several lakes to Wanda Lake, which is above tree line and surrounded by stark, rocky spires. Since it is an exposed

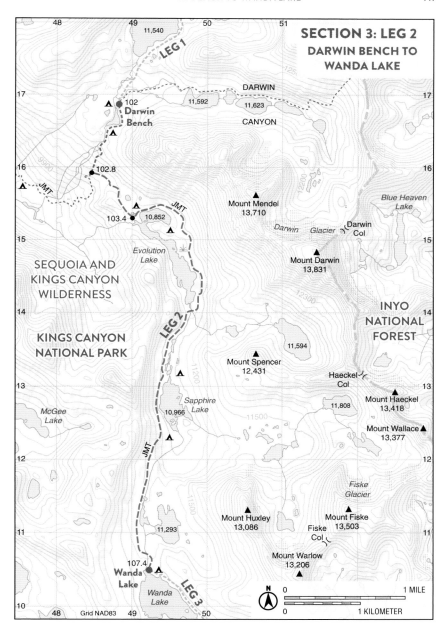

SECTION 3: LEG 2
DARWIN BENCH TO WANDA LAKE

Mount Spencer from Evolution Lake

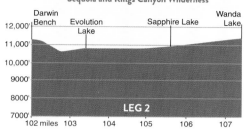

place to camp, it is not popular with JMT walkers, so it is a good campsite if you wish to camp away from crowds.

From Darwin Bench (**102**), a hanging valley, follow the stream southwest and pass some small lakes. The valley soon ends. Descend steeply, staying east of the stream; while you'll need to do some short scrambles, nothing is difficult. You can follow an unmarked trail most of the way; if you lose the trail, veer left (east) to meet the JMT. *If you are traveling south to north, from Evolution Lake follow the John Muir Trail northwest for 0.5 mile descending steadily to an obvious sharp bend to the left (southwest). Leave the John Muir Trail here and follow the light trail north up to Darwin Bench.*

At the junction with the JMT (**102.8**), turn left (east) on the trail and climb to Evolution Lake. Evolution Lake, one of the highlights on the John Muir Trail, is a popular campsite. But you can find sites away from the crowds among granite slabs north of the lake. Its popularity is deserved because nearby peaks are reflected in the waters of the lake and its satellite tarns. Mount Spencer at the head of the lake catches the alpenglow at both sunset and sunrise.

From the northwest corner of Evolution Lake (**103.4**), follow the JMT along the north then east shores of the lake. Cross the inlet stream at the south end of the lake via a long line of stepping stones. The trail continues southward passing west of Sapphire Lake then rises to meet the outlet of Wanda Lake. The area is barren and exposed with no shelter, but scenic campsites are available near the lake, which is named for one of John Muir's two daughters. This is the last suitable site for camping until past Helen Lake on the other side of Muir Pass at the end of Leg 3.

3 WANDA LAKE TO UNNAMED LAKE

DISTANCE: 4.7 miles
ELEVATION GAIN/LOSS: +530 feet / -1110 feet
TIME: 3½–4½ hours

The Sierra Grand Traverse continues following the John Muir Trail (JMT) over Muir Pass. The stone hut in the pass provides a sheltered spot for a break if needed but should not be used for overnight camping. The pass is named for John Muir, the naturalist instrumental in the creation of national parks in the Sierra Nevada. From the pass, the trail descends to an unnamed lake where there is limited

Helen Lake from Muir Pass

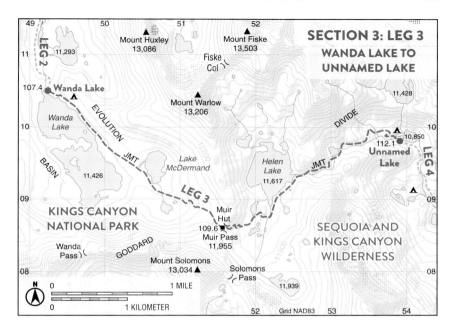

camping. More camping opportunities are available by descending farther into Le Conte Canyon (Leg 4).

From the north end of Wanda Lake (**107.4**), continue following the JMT southeast, passing close to Wanda Lake and then the rock-bound Lake McDermand. A final stony climb leads to Muir Pass.

A stone hut, built in 1930 by the Sierra Club, sits at Muir Pass (**109.6**). The hut is for day use only: Overnight camping and fires are banned. In fine weather the pass provides some great views, but in bleak conditions, the hut provides a sheltered place for a rest stop—other than in severe weather such as thunderstorms, when lightning could strike it. From Muir Pass continue following the JMT, which

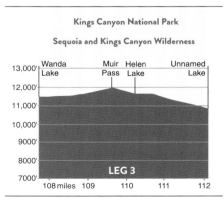

Stone hut at Muir Pass

heads northeast, switchbacking as it descends stony slopes to another rock-bound body of water, Helen Lake, named after John Muir's other daughter. Follow along the southeast shore of Helen Lake as you continue descending northeast. Pass to the southeast of a small unnamed lake to reach unnamed Lake 10,850 just above tree line. This is the first campsite since Wanda Lake. Sites are exposed and limited in number.

4 | UNNAMED LAKE TO LE CONTE RANGER STATION

DISTANCE: 4.3 miles
ELEVATION GAIN/LOSS: +50 feet / -2150 feet
TIME: 2½–3 hours

The John Muir Trail descends into the forested Le Conte Canyon. Breaks in the forest provide some views of the surrounding crags. There are numerous established campsites along the valley. Easy walking leads to the signposted side trail to Dusy Basin and Bishop Pass.

From unnamed Lake 10,850 (**112.1**), the trail heads southeast, descending to a grassy meadow beside the next lake where there are more campsites on marshy ground. From this area (**112.9**), the John Muir Trail now heads east, following the Middle Fork Kings River while descending steadily into Le Conte Canyon. You'll snag good views of the canyon from the trail. Enter the almost flat valley

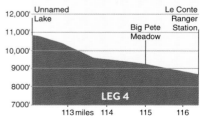

Kings Canyon National Park

Sequoia and Kings Canyon Wilderness

Middle Fork Kings River in Le Conte Canyon

floor as you pass through forest to a famous photographic point, a split granite boulder that looks like a giant mouth. Continue through alternating forest and openings, passing numerous campsites, to Big Pete Meadow. The trail stays in forest, skirting around the meadow, which has helped protect it. Please stay on the trail here.

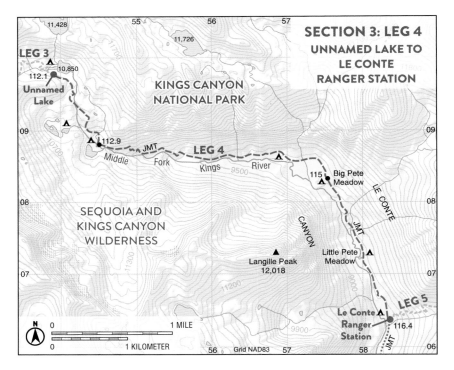

Continue southeast from Big Pete Meadow (**115**) in forest through the canyon and pass Little Pete Meadow to arrive at a trail junction near Le Conte Ranger Station. You'll find campsites in forest in many places in the valley; do not camp on any open meadows.

5   LE CONTE RANGER STATION TO DUSY BASIN

DISTANCE: 3.8 miles
ELEVATION GAIN/LOSS: +2680 feet / -50 feet
TIME: 4–5 hours

The graded trail to Dusy Basin is a long climb with many switchbacks. It passes some Sierra junipers and has appealing views of the creek cascading down steep

Exploring Dusy Basin

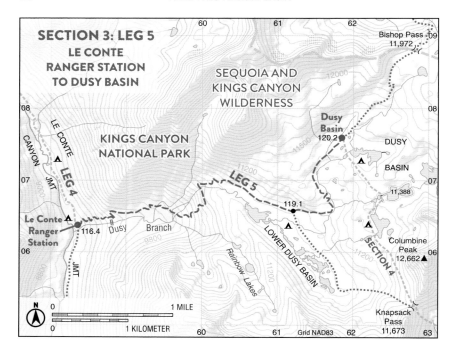

granite slabs. Leave the John Muir Trail at the Le Conte Ranger Station (**116.4**) by turning left (east) toward Bishop Pass. The benched trail switchbacks up quickly, passing some large, solitary juniper trees and has views of the creek flowing down steep granite slabs. After 2000 vertical feet of climbing, the grade eases as the

trail enters the hanging valley containing the lakes of Lower Dusy Basin. The marked trail heads southeast, passing close to the westernmost lake, then gradually swings left heading away from the lake.

From Lower Dusy Basin (**119.1**), the trail initially starts climbing eastward then swings northwest then northeast, and the section ends close to the large northernmost lake in Dusy Basin. From the 119.1-mile mark, you can take a

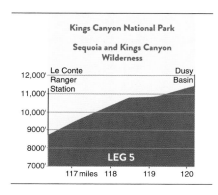

alternate direct route to Knapsack Pass (see sidebar, "Alternate Route: Direct Route to Knapsack Pass").

ALTERNATE ROUTE: DIRECT ROUTE TO KNAPSACK PASS

If not resupplying via a trip to South Lake, you can take an alternate route from Lower Dusy Basin direct to Knapsack Pass. While the traverse is then 1.3 miles shorter, you do miss the lovely scenery of Dusy Basin.

In Lower Dusy Basin (**119.1**), leave the marked trail when the trail starts climbing away from the lakes. Head southeast following use trails passing north of the lakes to the last lake before Knapsack Pass. To avoid willows stay well above the lakes. At the end of the valley continue to follow a use trail east then southeast climbing scree and rocks to Knapsack Pass (**121.9**, in Section 4, Leg 1).

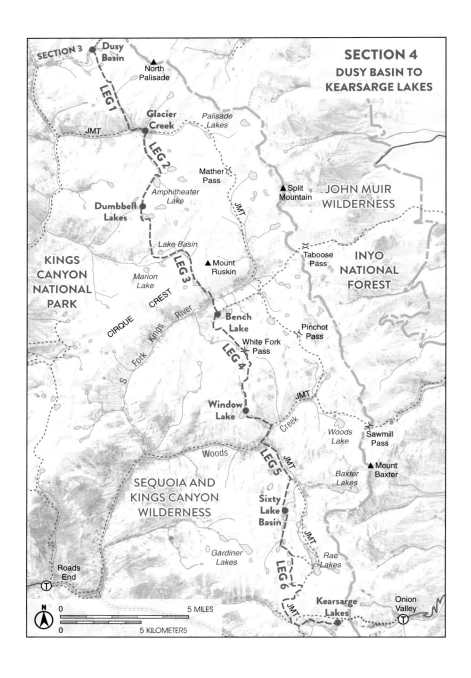

SECTION 3

Dusy
Basin

North
Palisade

LEG 1

Glacier
Creek

JMT

Palisade
Lakes

LEG 2

Mather
Pass

Amphitheater
Lake

Dumbbell
Lakes

JMT

Split
Mountain

JOHN MUIR
WILDERNESS

Lake Basin

LEG 3

Mount
Ruskin

Taboose
Pass

INYO
NATIONAL
FOREST

KINGS
CANYON
NATIONAL
PARK

Marion
Lake

CREST

CIRQUE

S Fork Kings River

Bench
Lake

Pinchot
Pass

LEG 4

White Fork
Pass

JMT

Window
Lake

Creek

Woods
Lake

Sawmill
Pass

Woods

LEG 5

JMT

Mount
Baxter

SEQUOIA AND
KINGS CANYON
WILDERNESS

Baxter
Lakes

Sixty
Lake
Basin

JMT

Gardiner
Lakes

LEG 6

Rae
Lakes

Roads
End

Ⓣ

JMT

Kearsarge
Lakes

Onion
Valley

Ⓣ

SECTION 4
DUSY BASIN TO
KEARSARGE LAKES

N

0   5 MILES

0   5 KILOMETERS

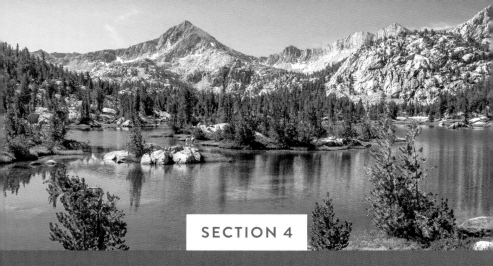

DUSY BASIN TO KEARSARGE LAKES

DISTANCE: 37.2 miles
TIME: 4 to 8 days
ON-TRAIL: 7.5 miles
OFF-TRAIL: 29.7 miles
ELEVATION GAIN: +12,360 feet
ELEVATION LOSS: -12,740 feet
LOW POINT: 8492 feet
HIGH POINT: 12,300 feet
MAPS: Harrison: Kings Canyon High Country; USGS: Mount Thompson, North Palisade, Marion Peak, Mount Pinchot, Mount Clarence King, Kearsarge Peak

PERMITS & REGULATIONS

Obtain a new wilderness permit for a South Lake entry from the Inyo National Forest office in Bishop if you take any zero days. If Cataract Creek Pass is blocked by snow, you may have to tackle some class 3 scrambling up bluffs.

LEGS

1. Dusy Basin to Glacier Creek
2. Glacier Creek to Dumbbell Lakes
3. Dumbbell Lakes to Bench Lake
4. Bench Lake to Window Lake
5. Window Lake to Sixty Lake Basin
6. Sixty Lake Basin to Kearsarge Lakes

ABOVE: *Sixty Lake Basin (Legs 5 and 6)*

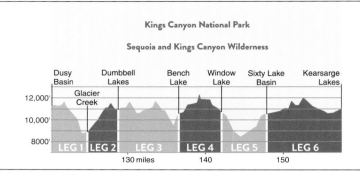

The notable features of this section are some long descents and ascents to cross deep valleys and high passes to visit scenic lake basins. Begin by crossing Dusy Basin to Knapsack Pass, and then make a long, steep descent to the John Muir Trail (JMT) near Palisade Creek. You soon leave the trail for an off-trail climb following Cataract Creek to Amphitheater Lake. An intricate steep route then leads to Cataract Creek Pass.

From Cataract Creek Pass, a descent on open slopes leads to Dumbbell Lakes. Crossing a sloping slab is the biggest challenge on this fairly straightforward off-trail route over Dumbbell Pass to Lake Basin. This basin has a reputation for its beauty; it contains numerous lakes, Marion Lake the most notable among them. Leave the basin by following an old, abandoned section of the JMT over Cartridge Pass to South Fork Kings River. The off-trail hiking resumes with a steep climb to the scenic Bench Lake then a crossing of two passes leads to Window Lake.

The Sierra Grand Traverse then descends to the JMT and follows it briefly, then an easy climb leads to the north end of Sixty Lake Basin. Filled with lakes and tarns, this basin is one of the jewels of the Sierra Nevada and to pass from one end to the other is a delight. The traverse leaves the basin by crossing another pass, Rae Col, to rejoin the JMT crossing Glen Pass. It then follows marked trails to end the section at Kearsarge Lakes.

ACCESS

This section of the traverse is accessible from the South Lake on the north end and Kearsarge Lakes on the south end.

North: South Lake

From South Lake, a well-maintained trail leads over Bishop Pass to Dusy Basin. The Bishop Creek Shuttle operates twice a day from mid-June until late August from the nearby town of Bishop to South Lake. An alternative is to have a food resupply stored at Parchers Resort (a storage fee applies), which is about a half-hour walk from the parking lot at South Lake via a hiking trail.

To travel from South Lake back to the traverse, from the parking lot follow the trail south. This rises steadily through sparse forest with openings providing some good views of South Lake to the first trail junction. Keep left as the trail climbs southeast following a broad spur. Ignore all side trails and continue to Long Lake where there are potential campsites. The trail follows the east shore of Long Lake, then climbs again to pass Spearhead Lake. Pass below Timberline Tarns and continue to Saddlerock Lake, 3 miles from the start (about three hours). It is another 0.6 mile to climb to Bishop Lake where you'll find numerous scattered campsites.

From Bishop Lake follow the maintained trail southeast, which soon starts climbing, switchbacking through a rocky region. It then heads south with more switchbacks that climb a steep scree slope leading into the pass. Sometimes there are snowbanks to cross before the pass. From Bishop Pass follow the well-defined trail southwest, descending steadily to join the Sierra Grand Traverse near the northernmost lake in Dusy Basin. You've gained 2890 feet in elevation in 6.9 miles.

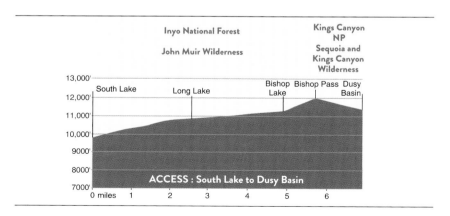

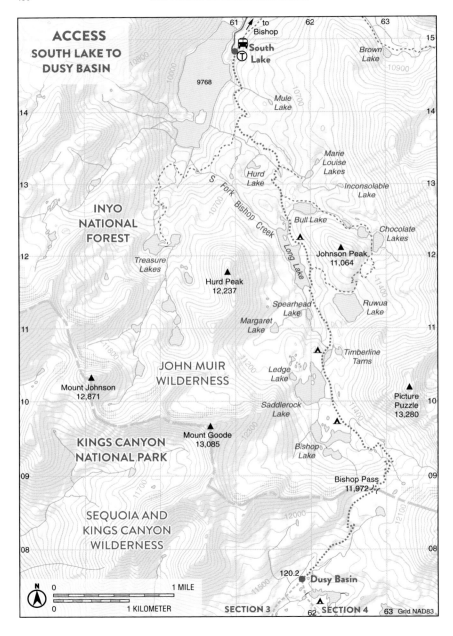

ACCESS
SOUTH LAKE TO
DUSY BASIN

to
Bishop
61   62   63

South
Lake   Brown
                  Lake

9768

Mule
Lake

Marie
Louise
Lakes

INYO   Hurd   Inconsolable
NATIONAL   Lake   Lake
FOREST
                              Bull Lake
                                              Chocolate
                        Johnson Peak   Lakes
Treasure   11,064
Lakes
                Hurd Peak   Ruwua
                12,237   Lake
                        Spearhead
                        Lake
                Margaret
                Lake
JOHN MUIR
WILDERNESS   Timberline
                                Tarns
                        Ledge
                        Lake
Mount Johnson
12,871   Saddlerock   Picture
                        Lake   Puzzle
KINGS CANYON   13,280
NATIONAL PARK   Mount Goode
                13,085   Bishop
                                Lake

                                Bishop Pass
SEQUOIA AND   11,972
KINGS CANYON
WILDERNESS

N   0   1 MILE
        0   1 KILOMETER
                                120.2   Dusy Basin

                    SECTION 3   SECTION 4
                    62   63   Grid NAD83

S Fork Bishop Creek

Long Lake

South: Kearsarge Lakes

At this point, most hikers will need to resupply their food and fuel, and the road at Onion Valley is reasonably close. From Kearsarge Lakes a short climb leads to Kearsarge Pass, then a long descent eastward ends at the road at Onion Valley, a loss of 2660 feet in 5.5 miles. At the trail junction near Kearsarge Lakes, follow the trail as it switchbacks northeast rising to another trail junction (**157.4**). Keep to the right and more switchbacks lead to the rocky Kearsarge Pass, 0.7 mile from Kearsarge Lakes. From the pass, follow the well-defined trail east. A long series of switchbacks leads down to the tree line. Continue descending, passing several lakes with campsites. Continue descending to the parking lot, 4.8 miles from the pass.

The parking lot has bear boxes, toilets, and a nearby campground where fees and bookings

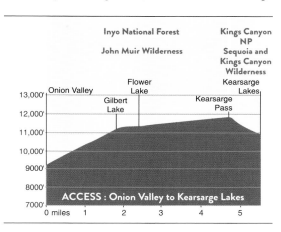

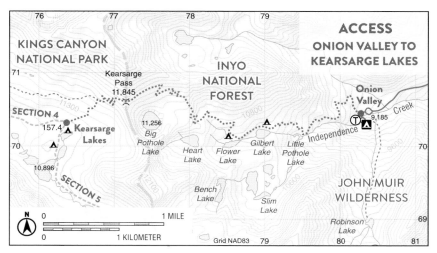

Kearsarge Lakes from Kearsarge Pass (Leg 6)

are required for overnight camping (see Resources). There is no public transport from Onion Valley to the nearby small town of Independence, which has few facilities. The only services are charter bus services and they generally leave around 3 PM and must be booked in advance. Charter services do change, and we recommend searching online for "Sierra charters east" to find current operators. Independence is 14.1 miles from Onion Valley. You can find overnight accommodations but only two small shops with minimal hiker supplies. Pre-place a resupply in Independence (storage fees apply) at the post office or the Mt. Williamson Motel. Otherwise you will need to take a zero day to catch the Monday to Friday bus to Bishop where there are more shops and some outdoor retailers.

Connecting Trails

There are not many connecting trails for retreat along this section of the Sierra Grand Traverse. The main retreat option is to head to the nearby JMT and follow it to an access point. From Dusy Basin to Dumbbell Lakes (Legs 1 and 2), the only viable option is to head back to the JMT and then follow trails to cross Bishop Pass and return to South Lake. From Lake Basin to White Fork Pass (Legs 3 and 4), you can follow the trail eastward from Bench Lake over Taboose Pass, but this involves a very long descent to a quiet road. A ranger station sits near the junction of the Bench Lake Trail and the JMT where assistance may be sought in an emergency. From White Fork Pass to Sixty Lake Basin (Legs 4 and 5), you can follow a trail over Baxter Pass, but again this has a long descent leading to a quiet road with little traffic.

Generally, after White Fork Pass, if you must leave the Sierra Grand Traverse, following the JMT and then the trail over Kearsarge Pass to Onion Valley is the best option. A paved road leads to Onion Valley and it is much easier to arrange transport than it is from the other less visited access points.

1 DUSY BASIN TO GLACIER CREEK

DISTANCE: 4.7 miles
ELEVATION GAIN/LOSS: +600 feet / -3080 feet
TIME: 6–7½ hours

The Sierra Grand Traverse crosses Dusy Basin then sidles around Columbine Peak to Knapsack Pass. From the pass, a steep descent leads to Deer Meadow beside Palisade Creek. The route briefly follows the JMT to Glacier Creek.

Dusy Basin (**120.2**) is a popular destination so there are a number of use trails and many scattered campsites. Leave the main trail and pass the northernmost lake in Dusy Basin on its south side then climb gently southeast up a rocky spur to a knoll. Continue south down the other side of the knoll to the outlet of Lake 11,388.

Next head southwest to easier terrain along the west shore of the most southern large lake. This is the last area in the basin that is suitable for camping. From the lake, head southeast then climb gently, passing through an area of large boulders. Continue toward the pass by following a series of ramps. The route crosses steep rocky slopes, and some routefinding may be needed to find the easiest way. Continue climbing

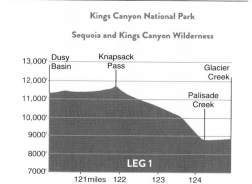

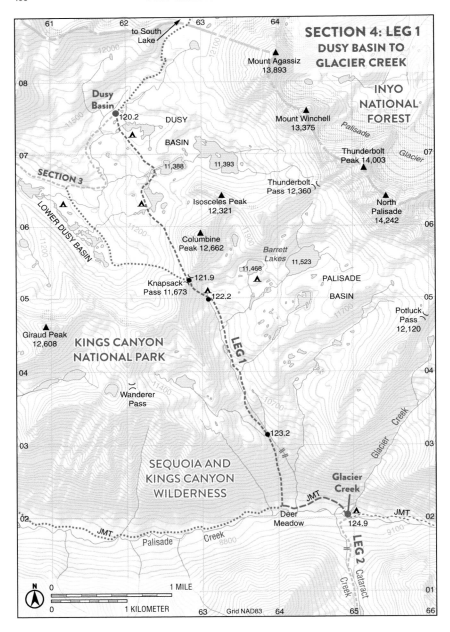

SECTION 4: LEG 1
DUSY BASIN TO
GLACIER CREEK

INYO
NATIONAL
FOREST

to South Lake

Mount Agassiz
13,893

Dusy Basin
120.2

DUSY

BASIN

Mount Winchell
13,375

Palisade

Glacier

Thunderbolt
Peak 14,003

11,388   11,393

Thunderbolt
Pass 12,360

SECTION 3

Isosceles Peak
12,321

North
Palisade
14,242

LOWER DUSY BASIN

11200

Columbine
Peak 12,662

Barrett
Lakes   11,523

11,468

PALISADE

BASIN

Potluck
Pass
12,120

Knapsack
Pass 11,673   121.9

122.2

Giraud Peak
12,608

KINGS CANYON
NATIONAL PARK

LEG 1

11400

Wanderer
Pass

10700

123.2

Glacier Creek

SEQUOIA AND
KINGS CANYON
WILDERNESS

JMT

Glacier
Creek

Deer
Meadow

JMT

124.9

JMT

9100

LEG 2

Palisade   Creek
8800

Cataract Creek

N

0   1 MILE

0   1 KILOMETER

63   Grid NAD83   64   65   66

Creek below Knapsack Pass

gently to enter the broad gully just below Knapsack Pass. A short climb on slabs on the left leads into the pass.

From Knapsack Pass (**121.9**), head southeast down the broad gully directly toward Deer Meadow. The easiest route is initially on the right side of the gully, then crisscrosses down the center to benches. It may take you about a half hour to descend from the pass, although if needed, the benches provide reasonable campsites.

From an area of potential campsites (**122.2**), follow the creek southward. Initially you'll find it easy going with short route diversions around small cliff lines. You'll encounter several small tarns and have nice views of the valley and Mount Shakspere to the south. As the creek descends, progress slows as the terrain gets rougher. Benches sometimes provide an easier route, but do not rise too far above the creek. Continue for 1 mile to cross a creek tumbling down from the unnamed lake to the northwest.

Below the creek crossing (**123.2**), descend about 300 feet into a small canyon just above the creek, then head to the right across steep slopes onto the open crest of the spur west of the creek. This provides views of the descent to Deer Meadow and the route across the valley to Amphitheater Lake. Follow the spur south, descending very steeply on open slopes of gravel and rock bands to Deer Meadow. Some routefinding is needed to avoid small bluffs. Cross the rough meadow to meet the John Muir Trail on the north side of Palisade Creek. Turn left (east) and follow the trail upstream. The trail veers away from Palisade Creek and then crosses multiple braids of Glacier Creek to an established campsite close to Palisade Creek. From Deer Meadow, expect to walk about twenty minutes.

2 GLACIER CREEK TO DUMBBELL LAKES

DISTANCE: 3.9 miles
ELEVATION GAIN/LOSS: +2620 feet / -620 feet
TIME: 6–8 hours

The off-trail route to Amphitheater Lake climbs a V-shaped valley. At one time a constructed trail existed on the west side of Cataract Creek, and you can still follow parts of it to a small lake about halfway up the valley. A steep climb then leads into Cataract Creek Pass. Depending on snow conditions, this can be one of the more difficult passes to climb on the Sierra Grand Traverse. Once on top of the pass, on the other hand, descent to Dumbbell Lakes is a breeze.

Leave the JMT at Glacier Creek (**124.9**) and cross Palisade Creek; sometimes logs provide a dry crossing. Cross the rough meadow beside the creek and head southwest for 150 yards to Cataract Creek. You could follow either side of the creek; the west bank has an old trail that is initially hard to follow but becomes better defined higher up. Follow the creek south climbing for 0.8 mile to a long,

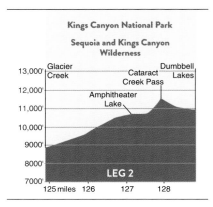

Cataract Creek Pass and Amphitheater Lake

narrow lake; this climb may take about an hour and a half from the JMT. The lakeshore is swampy and not suitable for camping.

At this small lake (**125.8**) follow the old trail along the west shore to the south end where the trail ends. Cross both inlet streams to the east side of the valley and then climb steeply southeast up the left side of the creek. The climb is a mixture of scree and gravel, then granite slabs leading onto a series of open benches below Amphitheater Lake. Continue south up benches to the lake. Campsites are readily available on the benches and near the lake.

From the outlet creek of Amphitheater Lake (**127.1**), head northwest along the shore to its north end. Follow the west shore, crossing bands of scree below cliffs, then leave the shore and climb the gravel slope on the right to a band of willows in a break in the cliff. Follow the willows through a shallow gully onto a small knoll and bench where there is a good view of the pass above. From there, continue southwest up the broad gully toward Cataract Creek Pass. There is sometimes snow at the top; the best route will depend on snow conditions. If the pass is blocked by snow, you can find a route either along the right-hand edge of the snow (which is sometimes a class 3 scramble) or up rock faces on the northern side of the gully. *If you are traveling south to north, from the pass head north for 50 feet*

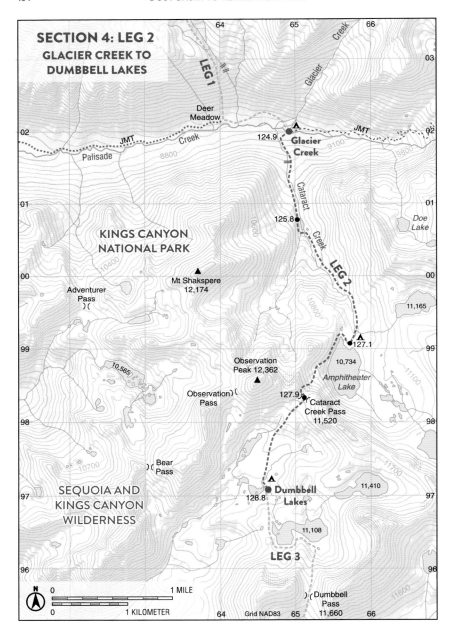

SECTION 4: LEG 2
GLACIER CREEK TO DUMBBELL LAKES

LEG 1

64

65

66

Glacier Creek

03

Deer Meadow

02

JMT

Palisade Creek

8800

124.9

Glacier Creek

JMT

9100

9800

02

01

Cataract Creek

125.8

Doe Lake

01

KINGS CANYON NATIONAL PARK

10400

10600

Mt Shakspere 12,174

LEG 2

00

Adventurer Pass) (

10800

11,165

00

99

10,565

Observation Peak 12,362

127.1

10,734

Amphitheater Lake

11,100

99

Observation Pass) (

127.9

Cataract Creek Pass 11,520

98

98

Bear Pass) (

10700

11700

128.8

Dumbbell Lakes

11,410

97

SEQUOIA AND KINGS CANYON WILDERNESS

97

11,108

LEG 3

96

11,600

96

N

0   1 MILE

0   1 KILOMETER

64   Grid NAD83   65

) (Dumbbell Pass 11,660

66

Sunset alpenglow at Dumbbell Lakes

then descend the rocky spur to enter the gully below the snow. *Descend to the bench 200 feet above Amphitheater Lake. Do not be tempted to traverse north along the bench because it leads into cliffs. Instead descend into the second patch of willows, then descend gravel slopes below the cliff to the lakeshore.* Cataract Pass provides a good view of the basin of Dumbbell Lakes and the route over Dumbbell Pass.

From the pass (**127.9**), head southwest, descending open gravel and grass slopes to the first of the Dumbbell Lakes. Veer left (east) to head south down gentle slopes toward two small lakes in the center of the basin. There are many suitable places to camp in the basin.

3 DUMBBELL LAKES TO BENCH LAKE

DISTANCE: 7.7 miles
ELEVATION GAIN/LOSS: +2820 feet / -3260 feet
TIME: 9–10 hours

To reach the next pass, Dumbbell Pass, you've got the usual climb up scree. The surprise, however, is on the approach to the base of the pass: Expect an awkward

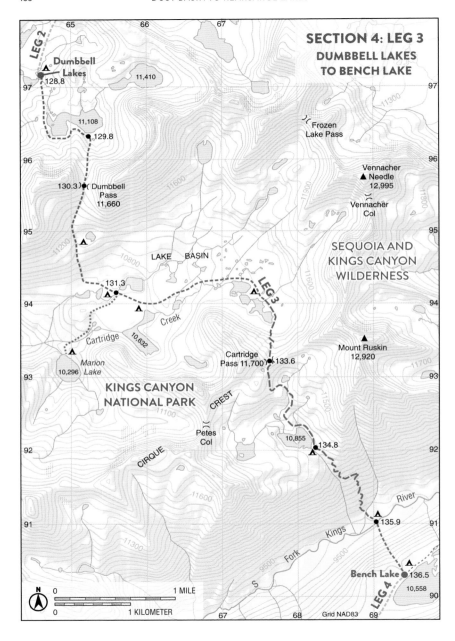

Marion Lake off in the distance from Dumbbell Pass

step onto a sloping slab as you look directly down on lake water. You can avoid this step by following the other shore of the lake, but it is a slow route with a long section of large boulders. The step is not difficult but requires some confidence. Lake Basin is scenic, and if you have the time, well worth exploring. From the basin an old trail leads up scree to Cartridge Pass and then descends to the South Fork Kings River. The old trail is faint in places and at times you need to be careful to follow it. This was part of the original John Muir Trail until 1938 when it was rerouted over Mather Pass. This route leads to a river crossing, which can be difficult at high water levels, and is followed by a steep climb through forest to Bench Lake, renowned for its scenery. While you'll find campsites where the Sierra Grand Traverse meets the western end of the lake, you'll also find a number of even more scenic campsites near the eastern end of the lake.

From the small lakes in the center of Dumbbell Basin (**128.8**), head south, rising up rocky slopes following a creek to the largest Dumbbell Lake, Lake 11,108. Follow the western then southern shores of the lake. When the shoreline heads north, just above the lake, a very short class 3 climb leads to a sloping slab that must be crossed with no handholds. Once past the slab, head east and round the spur to the base of the wide gully; this may take you about one hour from the small lakes in the center of the basin.

From the spur (**129.8**), climb south up the scree-filled gully to Dumbbell Pass. Sometimes there are bands of snow that can be either bypassed on scree or climbed directly. The pass provides a view of the striking blue waters of Marion Lake and there are even better views from a small bluff on the west side above the pass.

From the pass (**130.3**), descend on rocks, then grass to pass west of a small lake; camping is possible here. Continue south following a steep, wide gully filled with scattered trees. The way leads down to a pair of lakes in Lake Basin, which may take you about four hours from Dumbbell Basin. Pass north of the lakes and head southeast to the outlet of the next larger lake to the northeast. You'll easily find campsites in Lake Basin. The basin is another of the jewels of the Sierra; we had a rest day here and enjoyed exploring its many lakes.

To take a 1.2-mile side trip to see the incomparable blue waters of Marion Lake, leave the main traverse at the outlet of the larger lake on the northeast side of the basin. Head southwest to a saddle then descend south to two small lakes in the next gully. Turn right (southeast) and head downstream through open forest for about 300 yards, cross the creek, and rise over a low spur to the outlet of Marion Lake. Established campsites are available in forest on the northeast side of the lake. You will lose and gain 300 feet in elevation. Your return—after you've savored the lake, its jewel-like setting, and a view of the peaks beyond—should take about an hour.

Now back at the lake outlet (**131.3**), head southeast across Lake Basin to pass just north of Lake 10,632. From there, head northeast, rising gently into a higher

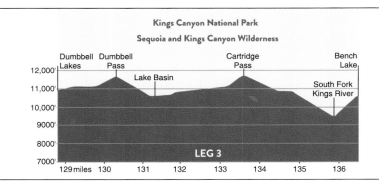

Vennacher Needle from Lake Basin

basin. Round the largest lake on its north side then follow a use trail southeast along the northeast side of the chain of lakes to the base of Cartridge Pass. Follow the unmarked trail south climbing into the pass. This trail was originally part of the JMT but is no longer maintained and some sections have fallen into disrepair. The trail climbs the scree just right of the rocky buttress, then when the scree slope splits, veers left to a bench above the buttress from where easier walking south leads up smaller scree to the top. From Cartridge Pass, Lake 10,855 fills the foreground, and beyond it across the valley is Bench Lake; both of these are your destinations in this leg. On the skyline directly above the right-hand side of Bench Lake is White Fork Pass, where you'll head in Leg 4.

From the top of Cartridge Pass (**133.6**), the trail turns left to follow the ridge crest northeast for 150 feet, then swings back right to descend and pass below the cliff in the pass. From here, head south. The trail is at times faint but is worth finding and following. It switchbacks down a very steep slope above a small lake and heads right toward a small saddle. Just before the saddle the trail swings back left (northeast) and traverses the side of a knoll to cross the creek below the small lake. From there, the trail is easier to follow as it descends a rocky spur southward to the tree line at Lake 10,855. Follow the eastern shore with some short climbs and descents to the lake outlet. Benches near the lake provide reasonable campsites.

At the southeast corner of the lake (**134.8**) an unmarked trail starts east of the outlet creek about 150 feet below Lake 10,855. You should be able to easily follow it but watch for some sharp turns. Follow the trail southeast, descending steeply in forest. When the trail swings east, you know you're about halfway down. The trail contours the slopes for 400 yards, turns sharply right (west), and then heads south, descending steeply to a wide flat in the valley. Walk through open forest across the flat to the South Fork Kings River. You'll find plenty of space for sheltered campsites in forest away from the river. *If you are traveling south to north, you'll see that the trail across the flat is very faint but becomes more obvious when it leaves the flat.*

Cross the river (**135.9**) and head southeast climbing steeply through open forest. To avoid cliffs, follow the broad gully, which becomes better defined as you approach the lake. Sheltered camping is available on the north side of Bench Lake.

4   BENCH LAKE TO WINDOW LAKE

DISTANCE: 5.6 miles
ELEVATION GAIN/LOSS: +1940 feet / -1800 feet
TIME: 6½–7½ hours

The majority of this leg is above tree line. There are no difficult sections, just plenty of the usual scree and gravel. You will obtain excellent sunset and sunrise views from many campsites along the way and will rarely meet anyone. The solitude you experience in this leg is a marked contrast to the nearby JMT, which crosses the same divide via a longer route to the east at Pinchot Pass.

From Bench Lake (**136.5**), follow the unmarked trail to the southwest end of the lake where the trail fades out. Continue southwest through open forest, then start climbing steeply to pass right of the cliffs. Sidle around the spur then swing eastward and climb steadily to a viewpoint on top of the cliffs overlooking Bench Lake. From the viewpoint, head southeast, rising gently to a rock-bound lake. Continue southeast, crossing over a rocky knoll to the next small lake. From Bench Lake, it will likely take you up to two hours to reach this point; you can find campsites on benches near the lake.

From the small lake mid-basin (**138**), continue southeast, rising to the last rock-bound lake in the basin. White Fork Pass is southeast of the lake and has a

Window Lake framed by cliffs

lot of steep, loose gravel on its upper slopes. To minimize climbing loose gravel, follow the east shore of the lake to the south end, climb southward up scree slopes to about halfway, then swing east and climb scree into White Fork Pass.

From the pass (**139.2**), descend steeply southeast on sand and gravel to easier slopes in the basin below. Veer right passing below small bluffs and contour around the basin to the broad saddle on the ridge to the southeast. From the saddle, continue contouring gentle slopes southwest then south toward White Fork Saddle. A cliff bars a direct route into the saddle. Descend left (southwest) along the top of the cliff until you can descend into the gully just below the pass, then turn right and climb the gully. Near the top, a very short descent leads into the top of the next gully and just above is White Fork Saddle. There are actually two saddles, but if you are traveling north to south, the second one is not noticeable. *If you are traveling south to north, from the more northern saddle, enter the gully and almost immediately climb a short ramp on the left to enter the top of a side gully that links around to White Fork Pass.*

From White Fork Saddle (**140.6**), an easy descent southwest follows grassy leads to the top of a cliff above Upper Window Lake. Either turn left to descend

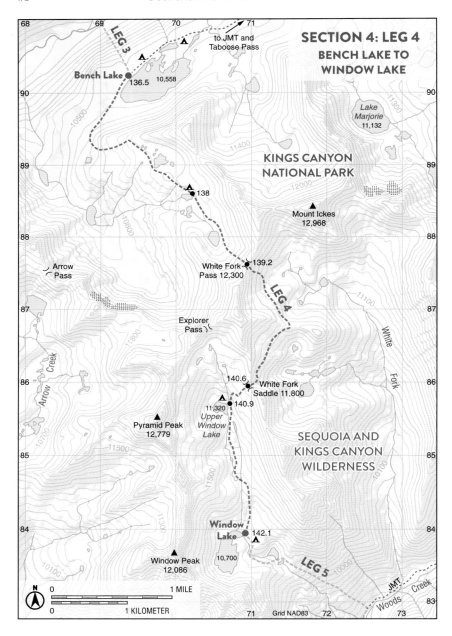

SECTION 4: LEG 4
BENCH LAKE TO
WINDOW LAKE

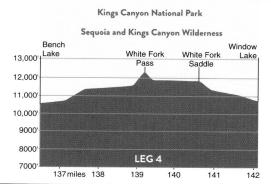

the steep rock-filled gully or turn right and traverse to a grassy bench that leads left down to the lake. Gravel benches near Upper Window Lake provide scenic, exposed campsites that have a wonderful view south of the next set of peaks and ridges. The alpenglow from here is often great although we have not witnessed it ourselves. On one trip, we camped here early and just made it into our tent before a large thunderstorm dumped heavy rain on us.

From Upper Window Lake (**140.9**), follow the wide valley and creek south. Slabs and open ground provide easy walking to where the creek swings east as it descends into a gorge. Follow the creek into the top of a gorge, and when the creek swings south, continue east about 50 feet to access a dry gully that parallels the main creek. Turn south into the gully, which provides an easy descent to the meadows beside Window Lake. The lake is at tree line and is semi-sheltered; you'll find established campsites east of the outlet creek.

5   WINDOW LAKE TO SIXTY LAKE BASIN

DISTANCE: 5.7 miles
ELEVATION GAIN/LOSS: +2210 feet / -2260 feet
TIME: 5½–6½ hours

A long descent on a wide slope leads to the John Muir Trail (JMT). Most of the descent is open, providing pleasant views of the route ahead. The trail then heads

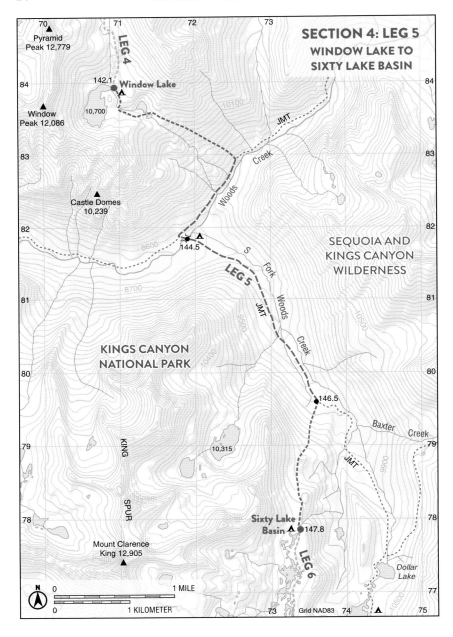

One of the many lakes in Sixty Lake Basin

to a suspension bridge over Woods Creek. A well-used, established camping area is near the bridge. From there, follow the JMT for the first 1.8 miles then it is off-trail walking to Sixty Lake Basin. The traditional route from the trail to the basin has been from Arrowhead Lake through Basin Notch to meet the lakes about halfway along the basin. The traverse leaves the JMT much earlier and is a pleasant climb leading to the north end of the basin.

From Window Lake (**142.1**), follow the outlet creek downstream, and when the creek swings east, cross to its southern bank. A steep route then leads southeast

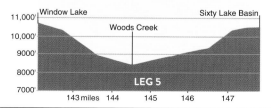

John Muir Trail near Woods Creek

and then east down a rocky slope to the next lake. Cross the outlet creek, continue heading southeast, veering away from the creek. Steep walking down mostly open slopes leads to the JMT; there are some small cliff bands on the way, and you can avoid these by descending short gullies. Before reaching the JMT, depending on which route you've chosen, you will encounter willow bands near the bottom; you may also need to traverse left to avoid cliffs just above the JMT. Turn right (southwest) onto the JMT and follow it downstream to a signposted trail junction. Turn left to cross Woods Creek via the suspension bridge to a large popular campsite with bear boxes.

From the suspension bridge (**144.5**), follow the dusty JMT southeast for 1.2 miles to cross a side creek. Continue along the trail for an additional 0.6 mile. You'll know you're there when you have a clear view of the high ridge and cliffs on the right.

Leave the JMT (**146.5**) and head southward toward the open gully on the side of the high ridge that rises toward Sixty Lake Basin. The straightforward climb is a mixture of grassy leads with some slabs and scree. At the top of the gully, pass through a narrow slot in a small bluff and contour across the head of a wide gully to benches north of the first lake in Sixty Lake Basin. It may take you up to two hours to reach this area, a little over one mile from the JMT. You'll find good campsites on the benches. This is a scenic place at both sunset and sunrise. While there is not as much alpenglow on the high peaks as at other sites, both the morning and afternoon reflections are stunning.

6 SIXTY LAKE BASIN TO KEARSARGE LAKES

DISTANCE: 9.6 miles
ELEVATION GAIN/LOSS: +2170 feet / -1820 feet
TIME: 8–9 hours

The Sierra Grand Traverse winds through Sixty Lake Basin, passing many lakes to meet a defined trail near the south end of the basin. The traverse leaves the south end of the basin with an off-trail climb over Rae Col. You can avoid some of the scree on this pass by following grassy leads to a gravel-filled chute. From the col, the route passes some rock-lined lakes and then joins the John Muir Trail (JMT) for the final climb to Glen Pass. From the pass constructed trails lead to Kearsarge Lakes.

The pretty and well-named Sixty Lake Basin (**147.8**) actually has more than sixty lakes and tarns. It's worthwhile spending some time to explore. Campsites in the basin are limited because flat areas more than 100 feet from water are rare. Continue south following the almost continuous chain of lakes for about 1.5 miles (about an hour and a half) to a small lake where the basin splits into two valleys.

Follow the eastern valley (**149.2**) to the next larger lake that has two inlet creeks; the valley again splits here. Pass west of this lake then climb alongside the westernmost creek to meet the end of a well-defined hiking trail. Turn left and

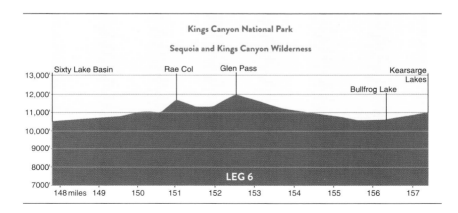

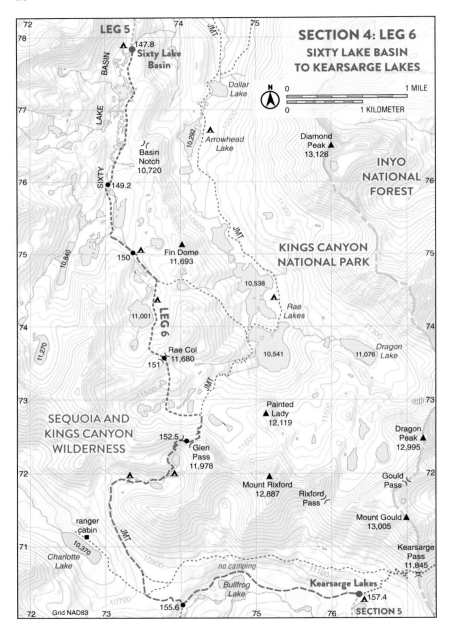

Near Rae Col in Sixty Lake Basin

follow the trail southeast, crossing the eastern creek and rise toward the next lake. Just before the lake, there is an established campsite below the trail.

From this potential campsite (**150**), continue southeast on the trail to the other end of the lake. When the trail starts climbing, leave it and follow a use trail south into the next lake basin where camping is possible. The use trail soon fades, but walking across grass along the eastern side of Lake 11,001 is uncomplicated. Rae Col is the dip to the left of what looks to be the lowest point in the ridge. The scree-filled gully to the southeast leads directly into Rae Col. While you can climb the gully directly, an easier route follows grass leads on the right side of the gully to the base of a black band of rock. Turn right to climb a long ramp to the bottom of a scree-filled gully that is hidden behind a rock buttress. You can then follow a use trail southeast up the gully; a final climb on a loose gravel slope leads into Rae Col.

From the col (**151**), descend gently south into a saddle and down to a small lake. Pass east of the lake, then descend more steeply to a chain of lakes in the

Lakes south of Glen Pass

valley below. The water in these lakes is often a deep shade of green instead of the more typical blue of other lakes. Turn east and follow the southern side of the lakes from where a short steep climb up scree leads to the JMT. Turn right and follow the benched JMT as it switchbacks southward climbing to Glen Pass.

From Glen Pass (**152.5**), continue following the JMT, which descends steeply to a large lake where you can find scattered campsites. The trail then swings west to pass a small lake. You'll also find numerous campsites in this area. Continue following the JMT as it crosses rocky slopes southward above Charlotte Lake to a signposted trail junction in open, dry forest. To the left (east), you could walk on a good trail directly to Kearsarge Pass, which may take about two hours. Instead keep to the right on the JMT. At the next signposted four-way junction, continue straight ahead following the JMT and descend to the signposted junction to Bullfrog and Kearsarge Lakes.

At the signposted trail junction (**155.6**), turn left and follow the marked trail eastward to Kearsarge Lakes. The trail rises a little, passes some small lakes, and skirts around the northern side of scenic Bullfrog Lake. Camping near this lake is banned; we saw two tents here, and to preserve the beauty of the lake surrounds, we encourage you to not do the same. Continue eastward through a mixture of small meadows and open forest to an unmarked trail junction close to Kearsarge Lakes.

Turn right (south) to the first lake, where you'll find established campsites. The lakes are a popular destination so numerous campsites are established in the area. This is a scenic spot with the jagged crest of Kearsarge Pinnacles towering over the lakes. While the alpenglow is special, the place is still pretty at other times of the day.

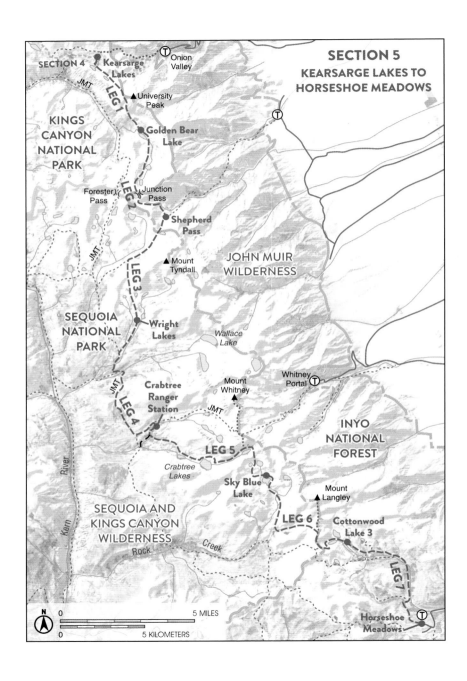

SECTION 5
KEARSARGE LAKES TO
HORSESHOE MEADOWS

SECTION 4

Kearsarge
Lakes

Onion
Valley

JMT

LEG 1

University
Peak

KINGS
CANYON
NATIONAL
PARK

Golden Bear
Lake

LEG 2

Forester
Pass

Junction
Pass

Shepherd
Pass

JMT

LEG 2

JOHN MUIR
WILDERNESS

Mount
Tyndall

LEG 3

SEQUOIA
NATIONAL
PARK

Wright
Lakes

Wallace
Lake

JMT

LEG 4

Crabtree
Ranger
Station

Mount
Whitney

Whitney
Portal

JMT

LEG 5

Crabtree
Lakes

Sky Blue
Lake

INYO
NATIONAL
FOREST

Mount
Langley

Cottonwood
Lake 3

SEQUOIA AND
KINGS CANYON
WILDERNESS

River

Kern

Rock

Creek

LEG 6

LEG 7

Horseshoe
Meadows

N

0   5 MILES

0   5 KILOMETERS

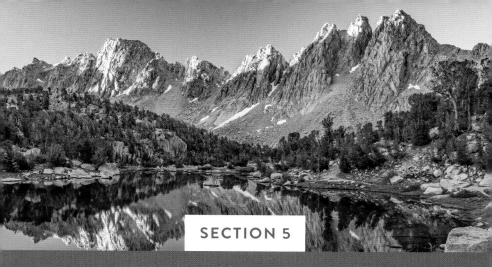

KEARSARGE LAKES TO HORSESHOE MEADOWS

DISTANCE: 42.6 miles
TIME: 4 to 7 days
ON-TRAIL: 17 miles
OFF-TRAIL: 25.6 miles
ELEVATION GAIN: +9430 feet
ELEVATION LOSS: -10,390 feet
LOW POINT: 10,040 feet
HIGH POINT: 13,100 feet
MAPS:: Harrison: Kings Canyon High Country, Mount Whitney High Country; USGS: Kearsarge Peak, Mount Williamson, Mount Whitney, Mount Kaweah, Mount Langley, Cirque Peak

PERMITS & REGULATIONS

Obtain a new wilderness permit for a Kearsarge Pass entry from the Inyo National Forest office in Big Pine or Lone Pine if you take any zero days.

LEGS

1. Kearsarge Lakes to Golden Bear Lake
2. Golden Bear Lake to Shepherd Pass
3. Shepherd Pass to Wright Lakes
4. Wright Lakes to Crabtree Ranger Station
5. Crabtree Ranger Station to Sky Blue Lake
6. Sky Blue Lake to Cottonwood Lake 3
7. Cottonwood Lake 3 to Horseshoe Meadows

ABOVE: *Sunrise on Kearsarge Pinnacles (Leg 1)*

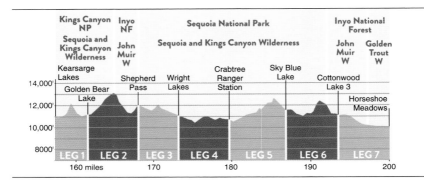

The final section of the Sierra Grand Traverse is higher in elevation but generally easier walking than the first four sections. You'll still need to tackle some scree-filled passes, but you can also revel in long sections of open walking across alpine meadows and basins. The route passes close to the highest point in the Lower 48 states, Mount Whitney, at 14,505 feet. You can climb the peak by taking a long side trip from Upper Crabtree Lake; for many this is one of the highlights of the Sierra Nevada.

Start this section by crossing the scree-covered shoulder of University Peak to Center Basin. Ahead is Junction Pass, the highest on the Sierra Grand Traverse; a long-abandoned section of the John Muir Trail (JMT) provides a fairly straightforward route to the top. The southern side of the pass shows why this section of the trail was abandoned: A very steep and loose, gravel slope leads into a tedious, scree-filled gully that eventually reaches the Shepherd Pass Trail. This is the last extensive scree walking until Crabtree Pass near the end of the traverse. Between is open walking across wide alpine valleys following a combination of tracked and untracked sections. From Crabtree Lakes, a complex route leads over Crabtree Pass, the last scree-filled pass, to Miter Basin. You'll then have an easier crossing over a spur of 14,000-foot Mount Langley before you pass through the popular Cottonwood Lakes basin to end in Horseshoe Meadows.

ACCESS

This section can be accessed from Kearsarge Lakes on the north end and Cottonwood Lakes on the south end.

North: Kearsarge Lakes

To join the Sierra Grand Traverse for Section 5 at Kearsarge Lakes, your closest access is Independence, on US Highway 395. From the town, it's 14.1 miles to the end of the road in Onion Valley, where there's a campground, and from there, it's 5.5 miles to Kearsarge Lakes. There is no public transport to Onion Valley—you must book a charter bus service in advance. They generally leave Independence around 8 AM and arrive at the campground around 9 AM. Other times may be available; check with the charter service. Charters services do change; we recommend searching online for "Sierra charters east" to find the current operators. Independence is a small town with few facilities. There are overnight accommodations but only two small shops with minimal hiker supplies. Pre-place a resupply (storage fees apply) in Independence at either the post office or the Mt. Williamson Motel, otherwise you will need a zero day to catch the bus to Bishop, which has larger shops and outdoor suppliers.

A large parking lot is near the end of Onion Valley Road; toilets and bear boxes are available. Continue through the parking lot on Campground Road to the Onion Valley Campground south of the main parking lot. Fees and bookings with Inyo National Forest apply (see Resources).

To get to Kearsarge Lakes, from the parking lot, follow the signposted trail to Kearsarge Pass, which is the bulk of the total 5.5 miles to the lakes. From the pass descend west to a trail junction. Turn left (south) and descend to rejoin the Sierra Grand Traverse at a trail junction just before Kearsarge Lakes. The trail on the right leads to Bullfrog Lake. Turn left and a short gentle descent leads to an established campsite near the first lake. Unmarked trails along the lakes lead to more campsites in the area.

South: Cottonwood Lakes

Lone Pine, on US 395, is the closest town to access the southernmost leg of the Sierra Grand Traverse. From there, it's 22.9 miles to the Cottonwood Lakes trailhead. Horseshoe Meadows Campground has two parking areas, named for the destinations to which they provide access. The traverse ends at the Cottonwood Lakes trailhead parking lot.

Lone Pine has some restaurants, overnight accommodations, and a few small supermarkets. To drive from Lone Pine, follow the road toward Whitney Portal for 3.2 miles, then turn left and follow the road climbing to Horseshoe Meadows and the Cottonwood Lakes trailhead. There are no bus services from Lone Pine to

Cottonwood Lake 1 (Leg 7)

Horseshoe Meadows, and the only public transit option is a charter service that you must book ahead of time. Charters services do change and we recommend searching online for "Sierra charters east" to find current operators. If you've completed the traverse and need to get to Reno and destinations from there, during summer a Monday to Friday bus service leaves Lone Pine early in the morning and runs north to Mammoth Lakes and Reno.

Connecting Trails

If you need to exit during Section 5, there are few intermediate retreat routes you can use. Generally the best option is to get on the nearest section of the JMT and follow it either north to Kearsarge Pass or south to Crabtree Meadow, then take the Pacific Crest Trail to Horseshoe Meadows. Shepherd Pass Trail (Legs 2 and 3) appears on a map to be a good retreat route, but it is a long and slow trail to a little-used road. In the Whitney Creek and Crabtree Meadow area (Legs 4 and 5) a trail heads east over Trail Crest at 13,484 feet to Whitney Portal. Backpackers without a Whitney Portal permit are not allowed to use this trail past Trail Crest. The Crabtree Ranger Station might be able to assist in an emergency (Leg 5).

From the Crabtree area, the best retreat is to follow the Pacific Crest Trail south then southwest over Cottonwood Pass to Horseshoe Meadows. If Army Pass is blocked by snow (Leg 6), follow the marked trail over the nearby New Army Pass, which holds less snow, and descend into the Cottonwood Lakes basin passing High Lake and Long Lake. If both passes are blocked by snowdrifts, follow trails south to the Pacific Crest Trail, then pass over Cottonwood Pass to Horseshoe Meadows.

1   KEARSARGE LAKES TO GOLDEN BEAR LAKE

DISTANCE: 4.1 miles
ELEVATION GAIN/LOSS: +1440 feet / -1260 feet
TIME: 5–6 hours

Kearsarge Lakes to Golden Bear Lake involves another scree-filled adventure. University Shoulder is not the lowest point of the ridge, so although a pass, it is called a shoulder. You can bypass it via a longer, less interesting alternative. Follow the trail east past Bullfrog Lake; from there follow the John Muir Trail southward for 4 miles, then head east just north of Center Peak either by following an unmarked use trail that is easily missed as it leaves the JMT in an open area with few landmarks or heading off-trail climbing through open forest east to Golden Bear Lake.

Head southwest along the west side of the first two Kearsarge Lakes (**157.4**). Pass the third lake on its east side and continue southeast along the valley to the fourth lake. Follow the northeastern shore to the other end of the lake and continue southward up scree in the valley. You're rewarded with good views of the route ahead. Nearing the top of the valley, veer right to climb the scree-filled gully to the western end of the pass known as University Shoulder. The final climb is steep. If there is a snow cornice in the gully then the rocky slopes to the right of the gully provide an alternative ascent route.

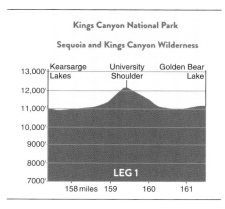

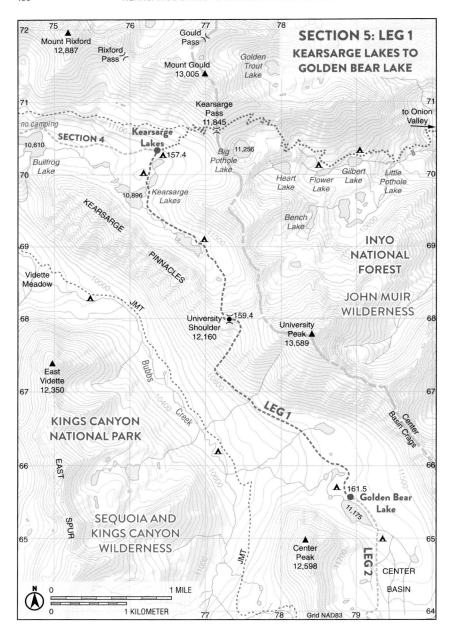

72   75   76   77   78
Mount Rixford   Gould
12,887   Pass
         Rixford   SECTION 5: LEG 1
         Pass   Mount Gould   Golden   KEARSARGE LAKES TO
                         13,005 ▲   Trout   GOLDEN BEAR LAKE
                                        Lake

71   Kearsarge   71
                        Pass   to Onion
no camping   11,845   Valley
         SECTION 4   Kearsarge
10,610   Lakes   11,256
                    ▲157.4   Big
Bullfrog   Pothole
Lake   ▲   Lake   Heart Flower Gilbert Little
70   10,896 Lake   Lake   Lake   Pothole   70
              10,896   Kearsarge   Lake
         KEARSARGE   Lakes
                                     Bench
                                     Lake   INYO
69   ▲11300   NATIONAL   69
Vidette   PINNACLES   FOREST
Meadow   10000   JOHN MUIR
         JMT   WILDERNESS
68   ▲   University ●159.4   68
              Bubbs Shoulder   University
                     12,160   Peak ▲
East   13,589
Vidette
67 12,350   10400 Creek   67
                                              LEG 1
KINGS CANYON   10600
NATIONAL PARK   Center
66   Basin Craigs   66
                             10600   ▲ 161.5   11500
    EAST   ● Golden Bear
                                         11,175 Lake
65   ▲   65
    SPUR   SEQUOIA AND   Center
           KINGS CANYON   Peak
           WILDERNESS   12,598   LEG 2
                    JMT   11700   CENTER
     N 0   1 MILE   BASIN
        0   1 KILOMETER   64
                        77   78   Grid NAD83 79

Center Basin Crags above Golden Bear Lake

University Shoulder (**159.4**) is an almost level section of ridge running east-west but is not the lowest point in the ridge between Kearsarge Pinnacles and University Peak. Do not be tempted to head to the lowest point because a cliff is on the other side and there's no easy way along the ridgetop to the shoulder. From the eastern end of University Shoulder head southwest and descend a gravel-filled gully, which is not as steep as the ascent, to scree-covered slopes below. When the slopes allow, veer left and follow the treeline southward to cross a creek between a small lake and the tree line. Follow the tree line southeast to more small lakes and soon after Golden Bear Lake. Good campsites are available near all of the lakes.

2   GOLDEN BEAR LAKE TO SHEPHERD PASS

DISTANCE: 6.5 miles
ELEVATION GAIN/LOSS: +2700 feet / -1860 feet
TIME: 7½–9 hours

Until 1932 the JMT followed this route over Junction Pass, and since then the trail has not been maintained. As a result, while some sections of benched trail remain, part of it is under gravel and scree. The route to Junction Pass is not difficult since the old trail can be followed most of the way. The highest pass, at 13,100 feet, on the Sierra Grand Traverse, Junction Pass provides extensive views. The descent from the pass is much slower: The old trail has vanished under very loose gravel and stone. A steep and slippery descent leads into a gully, then you follow a lengthy section of scree to a grassy bench known as The Pothole. From there, cross yet more scree to Shepherd Pass Trail. Once you join the trail, walking, while straightforward, includes a steep climb on a rocky track to the pass.

Follow a use trail along the northeastern side of Golden Bear Lake (**161.5**) until about 200 yards past the end of the lake. The use trail continues but leave it by turning right (south) to cross Bubbs Creek and follow a faint trail south through Center Basin. The old JMT stays on the west side of the basin and rises steadily,

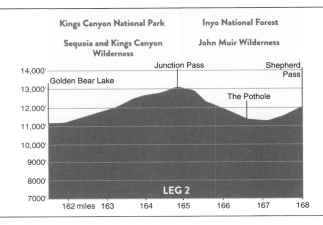

Scree-covered Shepherd Pass

passing above Lake 11,785. Camping is possible in many places in the open valley. The trail rises to a small tarn southwest of Lake 11,785, and this is the last possible campsite with water until The Pothole.

From the tarn (**163.2**), the trail then starts switchbacking up a steep scree slope. Continue to follow the old trail, parts of which have fallen into disrepair here, but it's worth following. The steep climb leads onto the narrow ridge from where you'll catch fine views of the John Muir Trail and Forester Pass to the west. Follow the old trail along the ridge crest southwest until the terrain steepens and then move eastward, climbing and switchbacking steadily on broken sections of trail to Junction Pass.

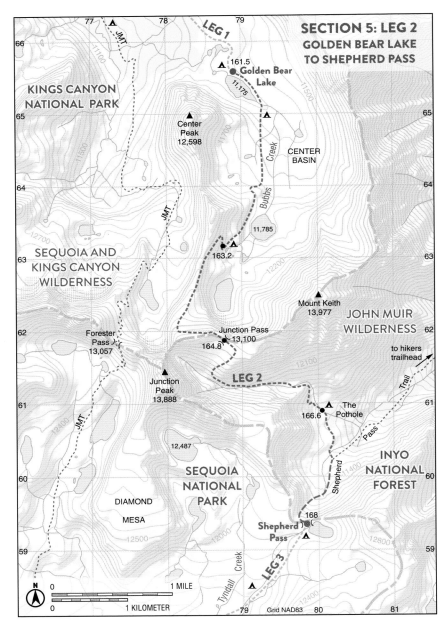

SECTION 5: LEG 2
GOLDEN BEAR LAKE
TO SHEPHERD PASS

LEG 1

JMT

161.5
Golden Bear
Lake

11,175

KINGS CANYON
NATIONAL PARK

Center
Peak
12,598

CENTER
BASIN

Bubbs
Creek

JMT

11,785

163.2

SEQUOIA AND
KINGS CANYON
WILDERNESS

Mount Keith
13,977

JOHN MUIR
WILDERNESS

Forester
Pass
13,057

Junction Pass
13,100
164.8

Junction
Peak
13,888

LEG 2

to hikers
trailhead

166.6   The
          Pothole

Shepherd

Pass

Trail

INYO
NATIONAL
FOREST

JMT

12,487

SEQUOIA
NATIONAL
PARK

DIAMOND

MESA

168

Shepherd
Pass

LEG 3

N

0   1 MILE

0   1 KILOMETER

Tyndall Creek

Grid NAD83

From the pass (**164.8**), continue southeast down open gravel slopes to a wide, gentle slope where the route swings southwest toward a deep gully. Take care descending the very slippery gravel and loose rocks on the steep slope leading into the gully. All evidence of the old trail has vanished. Turn left (southeast) to follow the gully. For about one mile progress is tedious and slow on loose scree until you meet a constructed section of trail, again a part of the old JMT. Follow the trail to a small grassy bench on the lip of a hanging valley. A creek surfaces here from under the scree, providing the first water since the tarn before the pass (at the **163.2**-mile mark). Head south on the old, eroded trail zigzagging down gravel slopes to a wide grassy bench above The Pothole. Camping is available on the bench.

From the bench (**166.6**), you could take one of two routes to Shepherd Pass Trail. One is to descend steeply east following a creek into the valley. The other is a more direct line steadily moving southward across scree-covered slopes. The route then crosses a scree-filled gully to meet Shepherd Pass Trail. Following either route takes less than an hour to gain the trail; we've indicated the route heading south on the map. Once on Shepherd Pass Trail, follow it southward climbing steadily into Shepherd Pass. Near the top, enter the right-hand gully where there is a series of tight switchbacks. The final section is a short way to the left, crossing a small gully that is sometimes filled with snow, then edge around a bluff to the pass. A lake and gravel benches near the trail close to the pass provide exposed campsites.

3 SHEPHERD PASS TO WRIGHT LAKES

DISTANCE: 4.3 miles
ELEVATION GAIN/LOSS: +560 feet / -1430 feet
TIME: 3½–4 hours

From Shepherd Pass, walking conditions become easier. Follow a trail initially, then enjoy some easy off-trail walking to cross a low pass into the wide, open alpine valley containing Wright Lakes.

From Shepherd Pass (**168**), follow the defined trail southwest, descending gently and crossing some creeks into the wide valley. Continue for 1.5 miles to

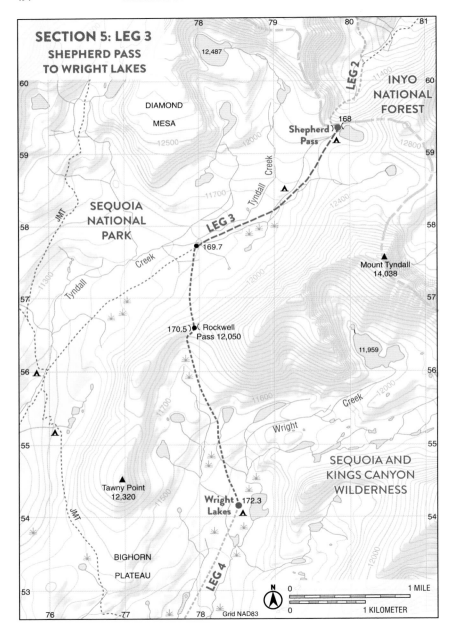

SECTION 5: LEG 3
SHEPHERD PASS
TO WRIGHT LAKES

LEG 2

INYO
NATIONAL
FOREST

DIAMOND
MESA

Shepherd
Pass
168

LEG 3

SEQUOIA
NATIONAL
PARK

Tyndall Creek

JMT

Creek

Tyndall

169.7

Mount Tyndall
14,038

170.5 Rockwell
Pass 12,050

11,959

Creek

Wright

SEQUOIA AND
KINGS CANYON
WILDERNESS

Tawny Point
12,320

Wright
Lakes   172.3

JMT

LEG 4

BIGHORN

PLATEAU

N

0   1 MILE

Grid NAD83   0   1 KILOMETER

Western Divide from Tyndall Creek

a creek crossing from where you can see a uniformly level, open slope leading to Rockwell Pass.

Leave the trail (**169.7**) and head south across grass and small stones toward the obvious saddle of Rockwell Pass. As you near the pass, a use trail provides an easy route through low-angled scree.

Rockwell Pass (**170.5**) is a broad saddle, and a short descent south leads into the wide, almost level valley of Wright Lakes. Continue south across open terrain for 1.3 miles, pass through an area of larger rock outcrops, and descend briefly to the largest lake in the basin. Exposed camping is possible almost anywhere in the basin.

Sequoia National Park

Sequoia and Kings Canyon Wilderness

Shepherd Pass | Rockwell Pass | Wright Lakes

13,000'
12,000'
11,000'
10,000'
9000'
8000'
7000'

LEG 3

168 miles | 169 | 170 | 171 | 172

4   WRIGHT LAKES TO CRABTREE RANGER STATION

DISTANCE: 7.4 miles
ELEVATION GAIN/LOSS: +780 feet / -1280 feet
TIME: 4–4½ hours

Most of this leg follows the John Muir Trail (JMT), which offers easy access to the southern edge of the Mount Whitney area. The only alternative to the area near Mount Whitney is a long deviation up Wallace Creek and over a pass to access the Mountaineer's Route to Mount Whitney (see Leg 5 for information on hiking to the summit). It is logistically easier to follow the JMT for a few hours to the next off-trail area.

From Wright Lakes (**172.3**), continue southwest following the open valley across Bighorn Plateau, crossing Wright Creek twice to avoid a swampy area to meet the JMT. Turn left at the JMT (**173.9**) and follow the trail southwest, descending to a crossing of Wright Creek, where you'll head briefly southeast. Past the creek, the trail again heads southwest through dry forest then swings east to descend to a signposted trail junction.

Cross the trail (**175.2**) that heads right to Junction Meadow and continue on the JMT to soon cross Wallace Creek. Pass a campsite, heading east briefly, then climb southward through an area of large rocks left from a glacial moraine on the west side of Mount Young. Rise into Young Saddle then descend southeast to

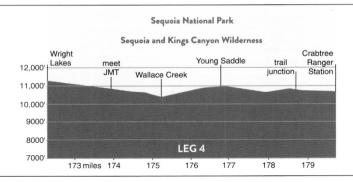

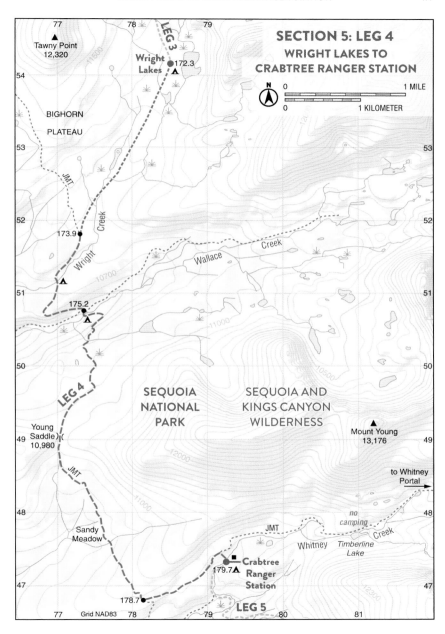

SECTION 5: LEG 4
WRIGHT LAKES TO
CRABTREE RANGER STATION

Expansive Bighorn Plateau

cross the top of Sandy Meadow. The trail then rises over a wide spur and descends gently to another signposted trail junction.

At the trail junction (**178.7**) turn left (east) toward the Crabtree Ranger Station. Follow the trail northeast for about twenty minutes, turn right at the next signposted junction, and descend to cross Whitney Creek to a large meadow. Camping in the large meadow is not allowed, but plenty of tent sites are in open forest on the south side of the meadow. This is a popular campsite with a pit toilet. The ranger station is in forest northeast of the meadow; rangers commonly check permits. While the meadow is signposted as Upper Crabtree Meadow, it is not technically in the Crabtree Valley.

5 CRABTREE RANGER STATION TO SKY BLUE LAKE

DISTANCE: 7.2 miles
ELEVATION GAIN/LOSS: +2450 feet / -1560 feet
TIME: 7–9 hours

The traditional route to Mount Whitney follows the John Muir Trail (JMT), which climbs eastward to pass Timberline and Guitar Lakes. Camping is banned at Timberline Lake, but Guitar Lake has many campsites and is popular with JMT walkers. The Sierra Grand Traverse follows a less-used route through the scenic Crabtree Lakes basin and skirts south of Mount Hitchcock. Lower Crabtree Lake is in a dramatic setting with steep cliffs towering above. Although sunset and sunrise are pretty at the lower lake, some will prefer to continue another two hours to Upper Crabtree Lake to camp to get an early start for a Mount Whitney climb. Mount Whitney is best attempted early in the day to avoid exposure to potential afternoon thunderstorms.

Crabtree Pass, the next objective from Crabtree Lake, is the last pass on the traverse without a trail. The climb to the pass is on the usual scree and the route is easy to follow. The descent on the south side is unlike the south side of any of the other passes on the Sierra Grand Traverse. To avoid multiple cliff lines, take a

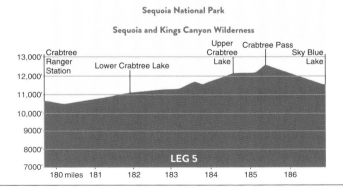

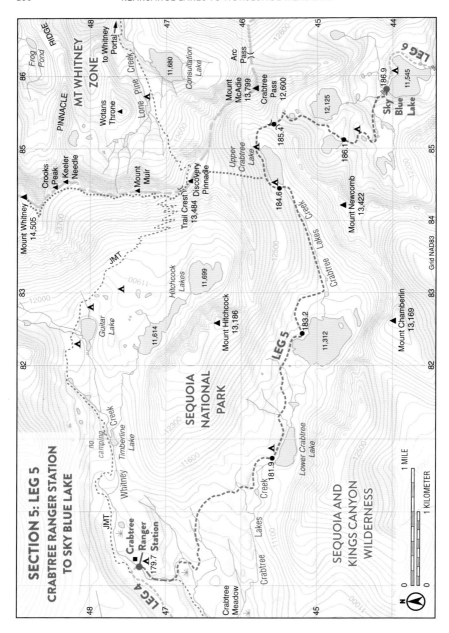

SECTION 5: LEG 5
CRABTREE RANGER STATION
TO SKY BLUE LAKE

Sky Blue Lake

complex winding route that passes a series of lakes to the aptly named Sky Blue Lake. In places, some backtracking may be needed to find a safe route.

From the meadow at the Crabtree Ranger Station (**179.7**), follow the trail that heads southwest along Whitney Creek and descend steadily toward Crabtree Meadow, which is not your destination today. After 500 yards, at a small meadow, leave the trail and skirt the meadow to its southeast side to locate an unmarked use trail to Lower Crabtree Lake. The trail is well-defined and initially climbs eastward, then heads southward through forest and scree to the tree-covered north shore of Lower Crabtree Lake. The forest provides sheltered campsites; expect to take about an hour to walk the 2.2 miles from Crabtree Ranger Station.

Continue along the north side of Lower Crabtree Lake (**181.9**). Head eastward from the east end of the lake past a small lake, then climb steadily over a low saddle to a sandy beach on the north side of Lake 11,312 in Crabtree Basin. Bypass the granite knoll at the east end of the lake (**183.2**) by climbing east-northeast up the steep gully on its left, and passing behind the knoll, and descending south back to Crabtree Lakes Creek. *If you are traveling south to north, at a small pond, turn right (north) and climb to pass behind the granite knoll.* Follow the creek northeast

Middle Crabtree Lake

SIDE TRIP: MOUNT WHITNEY

From either end of Upper Crabtree Lake, climb steeply north toward Discovery Pinnacle. The slope is known as "The Sandhill" because it is a tedious climb up loose sand and stony benches for two to three hours. From the top of Discovery Pinnacle, continue northwest, descending briefly to meet a trail at Trail Crest. You can avoid the climb over the top of Discovery Pinnacle by descending the pinnacle's east side, then following the JMT to Trail Crest, but note that this route enters the Mount Whitney Zone for which a special permit is required.

From Trail Crest, follow the descending trail northwest to meet the JMT at a signposted trail junction. Turn right and head toward Mount Whitney. The well-defined trail heads northward, passing Mount Muir, crosses the top of several steep gullies, then crosses a large scree field to the summit. You're now on the highest point in the Sierra Nevada, and in fine weather the view is extensive. There is a hut close to the summit. Return to Upper Crabtree Lake by reversing the route; you've just climbed and descended 2700 feet in 5.8 miles.

to Upper Crabtree Lake. You'll find an established campsite for several tents at the west end of the lake. This will be your base camp for your Mount Whitney climb (see sidebar, "Side Trip: Mount Whitney").

From the western end of Upper Crabtree Lake (**184.6**), follow a well-defined use trail along the north side of the lake to the eastern end, about a twenty-minute walk. There are a couple of small tent sites in this area. Crabtree Pass, your next destination, is to the southeast. The most direct route follows the lakeshore south then rises over a rocky spur into a scree-filled gully. Continue steeply up the gully to the pass. A longer and slightly less steep alternative climbs slabs on the spur left of the gully, then heads south along benches rising into the pass.

The descent from Crabtree Pass (**185.4**) is complex and in places several routes are possible. From the pass descend south into a gully and swing left to descend the gully to the northeast corner of a tarn. Turn right and pass along the north then west shores of a small lake, descend southeast a short distance, and continue southwest, crossing rough slopes with some ups and downs until you are due west of Lake 12,125. From there, head west into a low saddle above the next lake. From the saddle, head southwest to the lake outlet.

From this lake outlet (**186.1**), follow the creek south for about 200 yards, then veer left (east) to follow a wide granite ramp into a rocky basin with a small meadow and a small campsite. Follow the basin southwest past a tarn and continue south down glacial moraines into a rocky valley. Turn east and follow the stream to Sky Blue Lake. As you near the lake, the stream becomes a waterfall; descend on its west side. You will find an established campsite on the north shore of the lake.

6   SKY BLUE LAKE TO COTTONWOOD LAKE 3

DISTANCE: 6.6 miles
ELEVATION GAIN/LOSS: +1450 feet / -1900 feet
TIME: 5½–6½ hours

This off-trail section is enjoyable and not difficult. The route to Soldier Lakes involves some navigation, but it is not important to be precise with navigation as you will end up at either of the two Soldier Lakes. If you find yourself at the lower lake, follow use trails to the upper lake. The Sierra Grand Traverse then climbs onto the main spur that leads to Mount Langley. If you've summitted Mount Whitney, Langley will feel like a piece of cake.

You can reach this 14,000-foot peak via a side trail that leads to its summit. Follow the well-defined trail to Mount Langley down to Army Pass. In poor weather

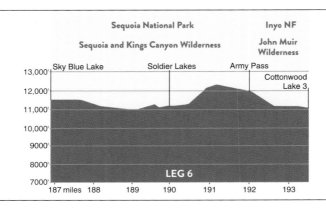

Waterfall in Miter Basin

conditions the alternative from Soldier Lakes is to follow marked trails south and then east to Army Pass. Army Pass contains an old unmaintained trail. If snow blocks the trail, an alternate route is to turn right (west) and rise to New Army Pass. While this pass is higher, it is much easier to bypass any bands of snow to High Lake; then follow trails eastward to rejoin the traverse near Cottonwood Lake 1. From Army Pass, the traverse descends into Cottonwood Lakes, the last lake basin.

Follow the north then east shore of Sky Blue Lake (**186.9**) to the outlet creek. Cross the creek and head downstream descending a ramp west of the creek to the slope below. Continue following a use trail southeast until it peters out in the flat valley of Miter Basin. Cross to the east side of the basin, continue south, and look for the use trail that starts up again near some small lakes. Follow it south 600 yards to where the trail descends into a dry gully.

At the top of the gully (**189**), leave the trail and continue south across the hillside, rising steadily to cross the southwestern spur of The Major General. Swing around to the southeast, rising to a small lake. Descend its outlet creek, then climb in forest to Upper Soldier Lake. (For an alternative route from Miter Basin, leave the use trail at the same place, mile 189, and head south, staying at the same height to the saddle northwest of Lower Soldier Lake). A use trail then leads east down to Lower Soldier Lake. Once you arrive at the lower lake, you can

Tarn in Miter Basin

follow unmarked trails to the Upper Soldier Lake. Campsites are available near both Soldier Lakes.

From Upper Soldier Lake (**190**), head northeast following the valley. This heads into the gully from where a switchbacking use trail climbs steeply eastward onto the southern ridge of Mount Langley. Near the top of the ridge, leave the trail and head southeast across open slopes to meet the hiking trail to Mount Langley. Allow some time for a side trip to the summit of the southernmost "fourteener" in the range.

Mount Langley has extensive views and is one of the easiest 14,000-foot peaks to climb in the Sierra Nevada as the trail is not very rocky and is a steady climb with few steep sections. Follow the clearly defined trail up the ridge northward to the summit. Return the same way. From the traverse, you'll gain 1530 feet to the 14,026-foot summit in this 3-mile round-trip. Count on at least two and a half hours to climb the peak and descend back to the trail.

Continue on the main route (**191.1**) by following the trail to Mount Langley south then southeast to meet a trail in the broad saddle of Army Pass.

From the pass (**192**) head east and follow the trail that descends toward Cottonwood Lake 4. This trail is no longer maintained, but with care it is still negotiable as long as there is minimal snow over the trail. One section has been damaged by a landslide, requiring a crossing of a narrow ledge. Continue descending to a series of switchbacks that leads to the west end of Lake 4. Follow a defined trail along the north shore to the outlet creek at the eastern end. The trail continues southeast descending to Lake 3. Cottonwood Lakes are a popular hiking destination and as a result a network of trails encircles the lakes.

7 COTTONWOOD LAKE 3 TO HORSESHOE MEADOWS

DISTANCE: 6.5 miles
ELEVATION GAIN/LOSS: +50 feet / -1110 feet
TIME: 2½–3 hours

The final section is an easy walk following well-used, constructed trails to a parking lot. Expect to meet many hikers ascending since Cottonwood Lakes is a popular area. The route for the Sierra Grand Traverse is the shortest through the area.

Cottonwood Lake 1

At the first junction near Lake 3 (**193.5**), head left (southeast), rising gently to pass close to an unnamed lake on its southwest shore. This is one of the largest lakes in the basin and it's surprising it was not named. Continue across an open meadow, then through open forest to a trail junction. Campsites are readily available anywhere in this region. To protect the grassy meadows, select sites within the tree line. Follow the hiking trail east as it descends steadily to a trail junction.

The trail on the right (**194.5**) leads south to trails that connect to New Army Pass. Continue straight ahead ignoring other trails as the main trail swings southward to cross Cottonwood Creek. The wide trail is well used and provides easy

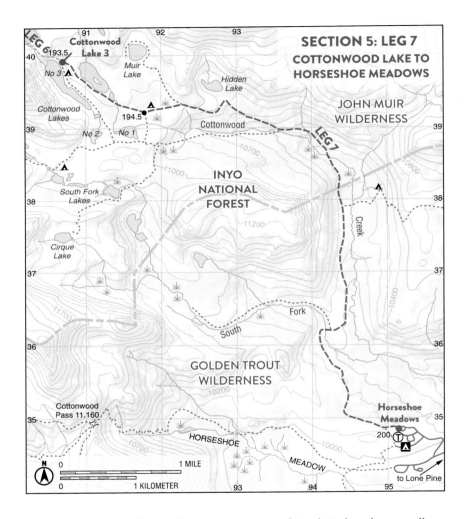

walking south through open forest to a crossing of South Fork and eventually to the Cottonwood Lakes parking lot in Horseshoe Meadows.

The parking lot is the end (or the beginning) of the Sierra Grand Traverse (**200**).

Congratulations! You made it to the end! Celebrate your "grand finale" with a hot shower and a real meal that is not trail food! Be proud of your accomplish-

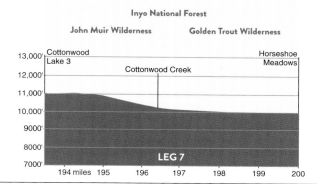

ment, as this traverse is a challenging backpacking trip. Memories of the rugged mountain vistas—where you ascended and descended all those scree-filled passes, and those of the many beautiful lake basins, where you sat watching the evening alpenglow and admired beautiful reflections in still alpine lakes—will last a lifetime.

If this is your starting point, you have an adventure ahead with so much to look forward to and experience!

ACKNOWLEDGMENTS

Thanks to everyone who encouraged us to continue creating guidebooks. We would like to acknowledge the use of the USGS maps as a base from which to draw maps. We would also like to thank Steve Roper for his book *Sierra High Route: Traversing Timberline Country*, which inspired us to follow his route and walk off-trail in the Sierra Nevada, which in turn led to a lot of research and more visits to the range that resulted in the featured traverse.

We are grateful to our publisher Mountaineers Books for believing in the opportunities this traverse presents hikers who wish to explore the High Sierra. Thank you especially to editor in chief Kate Rogers, designer Jen Grable, project editor Laura Shauger, copy editor Ginger Oppenheimer, and proofreaders Joeth Zucco and Debbie Greenberg.

Moonrise near Glen Pass (Section 4)

RESOURCES

NATIONAL FORESTS

**Big Pine: Ancient Bristlecone Pine
Forest Visitor Center**
White Mountain Road
Highway 168 from Big Pine, CA
(760) 873-2500

**Bishop: White Mountain Public Lands
Information Center**
798 N. Main St.
Bishop, CA 93514
(760) 873-2500

Inyo National Forest
www.fs.usda.gov/inyo
351 Pacu Lane, Suite 200
Bishop, CA 93514
(760) 873-2400

**Lone Pine: Eastern Sierra Interagency
Visitor Center**
US Highway 395 and SR 136
Lone Pine, CA 93545
(760) 876-6200

**Mammoth: Mammoth Lakes
Welcome Center**
2510 Hwy 203
Mammoth Lakes, CA 93546
(760) 924-5500

Sierra National Forest
www.fs.usda.gov/sierra

NATIONAL PARKS

**Sequoia and Kings Canyon
National Park**
www.nps.gov/seki
Permits: www.nps.gov/seki/planyour
visit/wilderness_permits.htm
(559) 565-3341

Yosemite National Park
www.nps.gov/yose
Permits: www.nps.gov/yose/plan
yourvisit/wpres.htm
(209) 372-0200

Clouds at Sixty Lake Basin (Section 4)

WILDERNESS AREAS

Ansel Adams Wilderness
Administered by Inyo
National Forest
www.fs.usda.gov/recarea/inyo
/recarea/?recid=21874

Golden Trout Wilderness
Administered by Sequoia and Inyo
National Forests
www.fs.usda.gov/recarea/sequoia
/recarea/?recid=79567

John Muir Wilderness
Administered by Inyo National
Forest
www.fs.usda.gov/recarea/inyo
/recarea/?recid=21875

Sequoia and Kings Canyon Wilderness
Administered by Sequoia and Kings
Canyon National Park
www.nps.gov/seki/planyourvisit
/wilderness.htm

Yosemite Wilderness
Administered by Yosemite National
Park
www.nps.gov/yose/planyourvisit
/yosemitewilderness.htm

PERMITS

Inyo National Forest
www.fs.usda.gov/main/inyo
/passes-permits/recreation

Ready for Wildfire
www.readyforwildfire.org/permits
/campfire-permit

Yosemite National Park
www.nps.gov/yose/planyourvisit
/permitstations.htm

MAPS

Tom Harrison Maps
https://tomharrisonmaps.com

US Geological Survey (USGS)
www.usgs.gov

NONPROFIT ORGANIZATIONS

Eastern Sierra Interpretive Association
https://sierraforever.org

Eastern Sierra Land Trust
www.eslt.org

Friends of the Inyo
https://friendsoftheinyo.org

Nature Bridge
https://naturebridge.org

Yosemite Conservancy
https://yosemite.org

TRANSIT

Eastern Sierra Transit (ESTA)
www.estransit.com

Sierra Nevada Shuttles
https://climber.org/data/shuttles
.html

Mammoth Lakes Basin Trolley
www.estransit.com/routes-schedule
/seasonal/lakes-basin-trolley

Yosemite Area Regional Transportation System (YARTS)
https://yarts.com

OTHER HELPFUL INFORMATION

High Sierra Topics
www.highsierratopix.com

Mammoth Lakes snow gauge
www.mammothmountain.com
/mountain/winter-weather

US Customs
www.cbp.gov

Yosemite Hospitality (concessionaire)
www.travelyosemite.com

RESUPPLY & ACCOMMODATIONS

Mt. Williamson Motel
www.mtwilliamsonmotel.com
515 S. Edwards St.
Independence, CA 93526
(760) 878-2121

Onion Valley Campground
www.recreation.gov/camping
/campgrounds/232077

Pack Outfitters and Stations
www.fs.usda.gov/Internet/FSE
_DOCUMENTS/fseprd550775.pdf

Parchers Resort
www.parchersresort.net
(760) 873-4177

Red's Meadow Resort
www.redsmeadow.com
(760) 934-2345

INDEX

Meadow west of North Glacier Pass (Section 1)

ABOUT THE AUTHORS

John and Monica Chapman are well-known hikers (bushwalkers) in Australia and together are the authors of fifteen hiking guides to that country. Some of their better-known books are *South West Tasmania, Cradle Mountain Lake St Clair and Walls of Jerusalem National Parks, Larapinta Trail,* and the *Australian Alps Walking Track.* Over four decades, they have written hundreds of articles about hiking for newspapers and outdoor magazines. The Chapmans have traveled extensively around the world and walked in many of the major mountain ranges. John has served as a trekking guide in the Himalayas and climbed some of the lesser peaks of the range. He is also a keen photographer and has been granted numerous international awards, including Grand Master of the Photographic Society of America.

After becoming a hiking and cross-country skiing leader, Monica helped run these leadership courses and was on the Bushwalking and Mountaincraft Training Advisory Board. She was president of Bushwalking Victoria, the umbrella organization for hiking clubs, and served eleven years as chair of Bush Search and Rescue Victoria (BSAR), a role she recently returned to as co-chair.

The Chapmans honed their wilderness skills hiking for weeks on end in Tasmania. Both Tasmania and the Sierra Nevada have many lakes and rugged peaks. However, they fell in love with the Sierra Nevada when they visited because it is more extensive, features more lakes and higher peaks, and has a more stable summer weather pattern. On their first visit they followed the Sierra High Route, and after much research, they returned to hike the route featured in this guide, a high-level traverse along the grandest section of the Sierra.

MOUNTAINEERS BOOKS

SKIPSTONE BRAIDED RIVER

recreation · lifestyle · conservation

MOUNTAINEERS BOOKS, including its two imprints, Skipstone and Braided River, is a leading publisher of quality outdoor recreation, sustainability, and conservation titles. As a 501(c)(3) nonprofit, we are committed to supporting the environmental and educational goals of our organization by providing expert information on human-powered adventure, sustainable practices at home and on the trail, and preservation of wilderness.

Our publications are made possible through the generosity of donors, and through sales of more than 700 titles on outdoor recreation, sustainable lifestyle, and conservation. To donate, purchase books, or learn more, visit us online:

MOUNTAINEERS BOOKS
1001 SW Klickitat Way, Suite 201 • Seattle, WA 98134
800-553-4453 • mbooks@mountaineersbooks.org • www.mountaineersbooks.org

An independent nonprofit publisher since 1960

 Mountaineers Books is proud to support the Leave No Trace Center for Outdoor Ethics, whose mission is to promote and inspire responsible outdoor recreation through education, research, and partnerships. The Leave No Trace program is focused specifically on human-powered (nonmotorized) recreation. For more information, visit www.lnt.org.

YOU MAY ALSO LIKE: